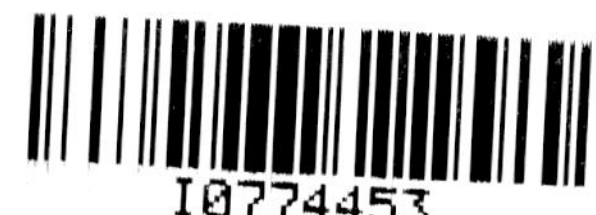

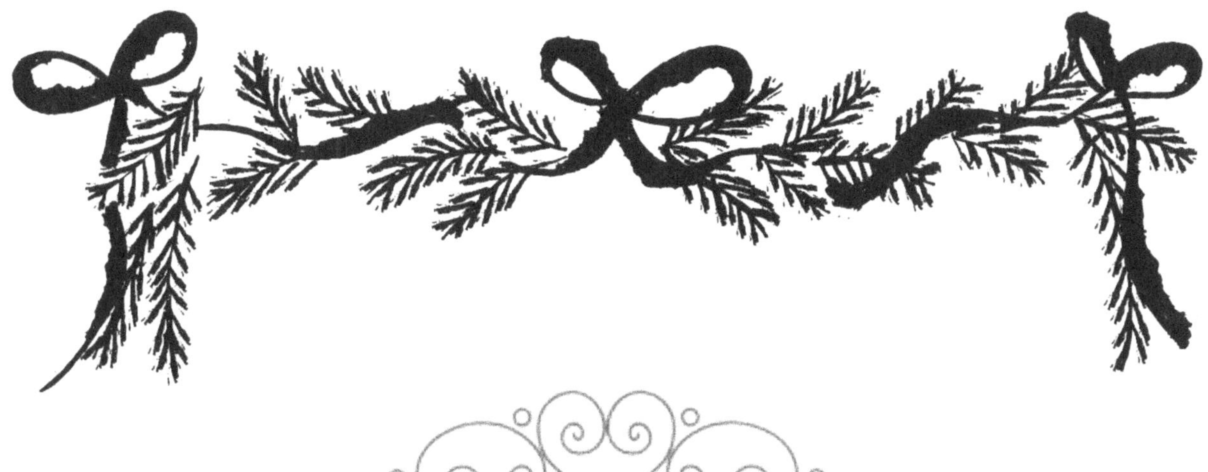

flower Belongs To Page

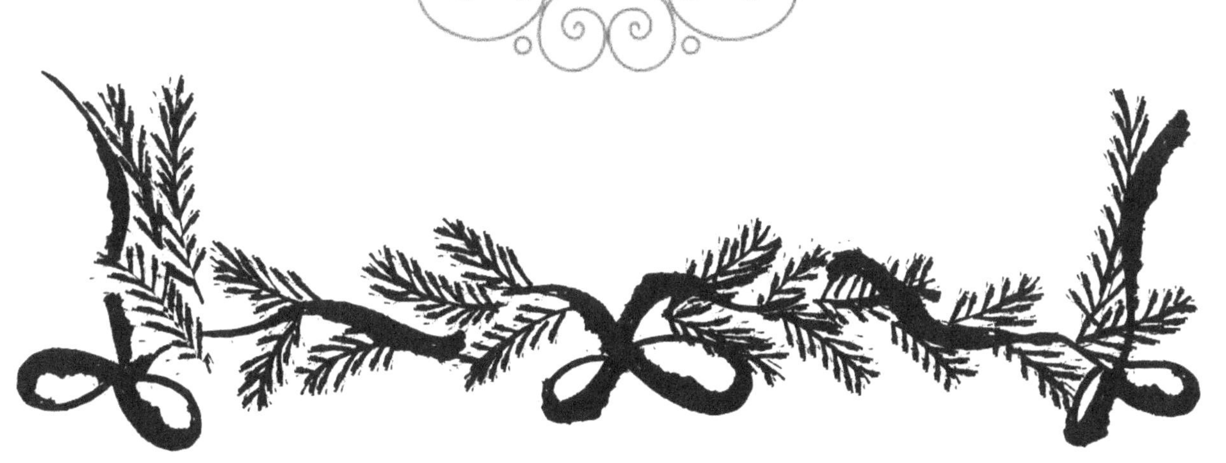

Color Test Page

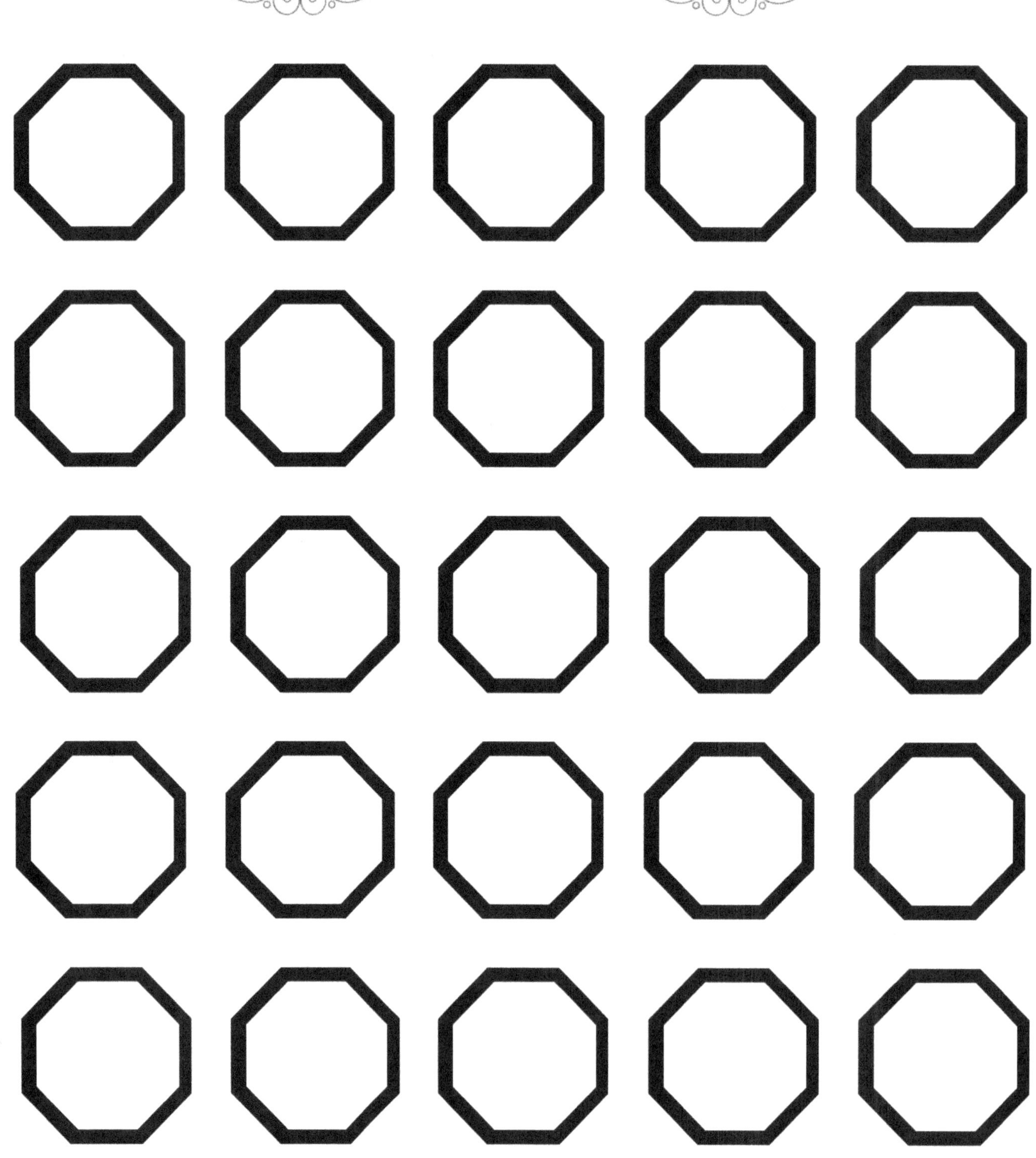

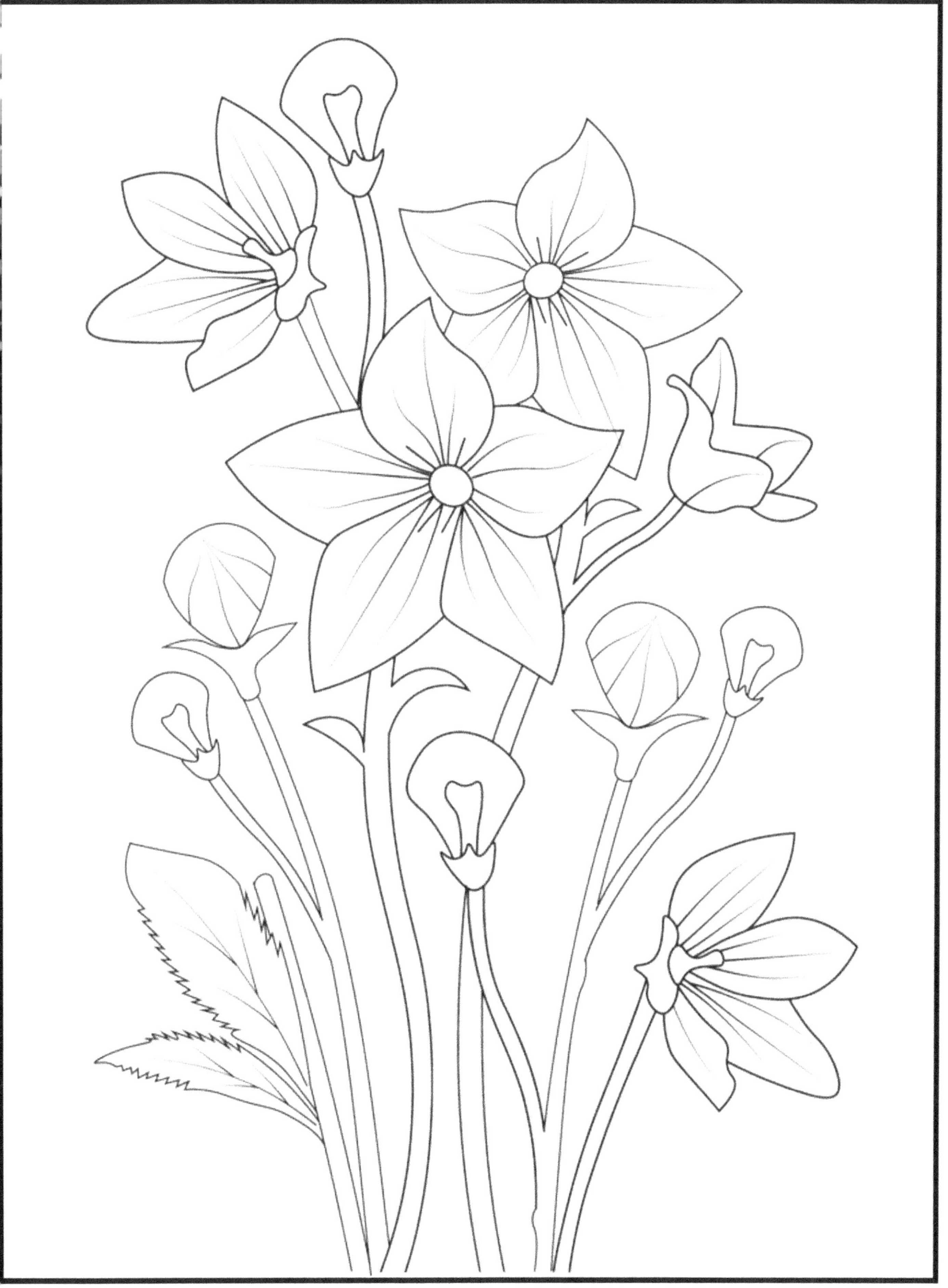

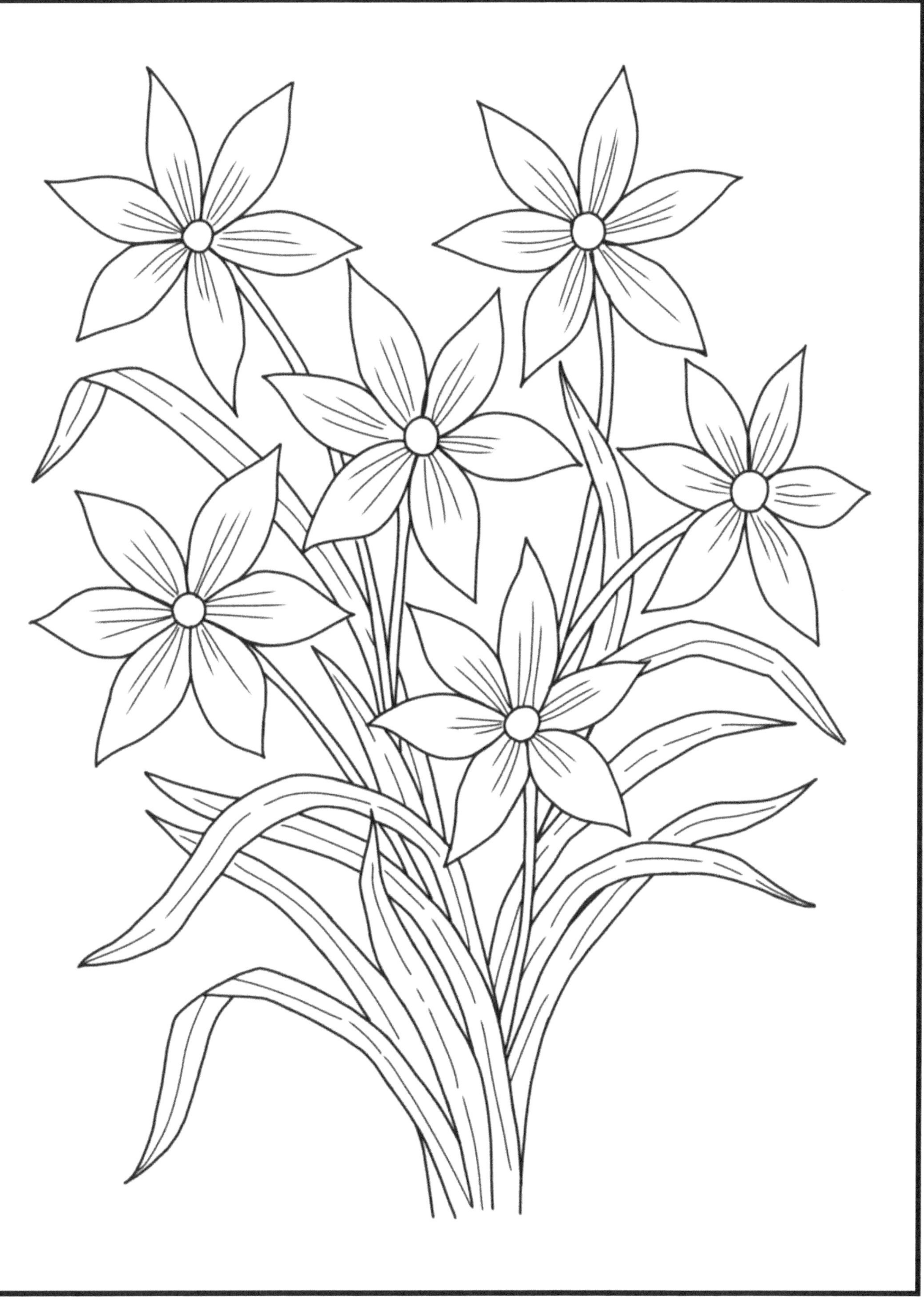

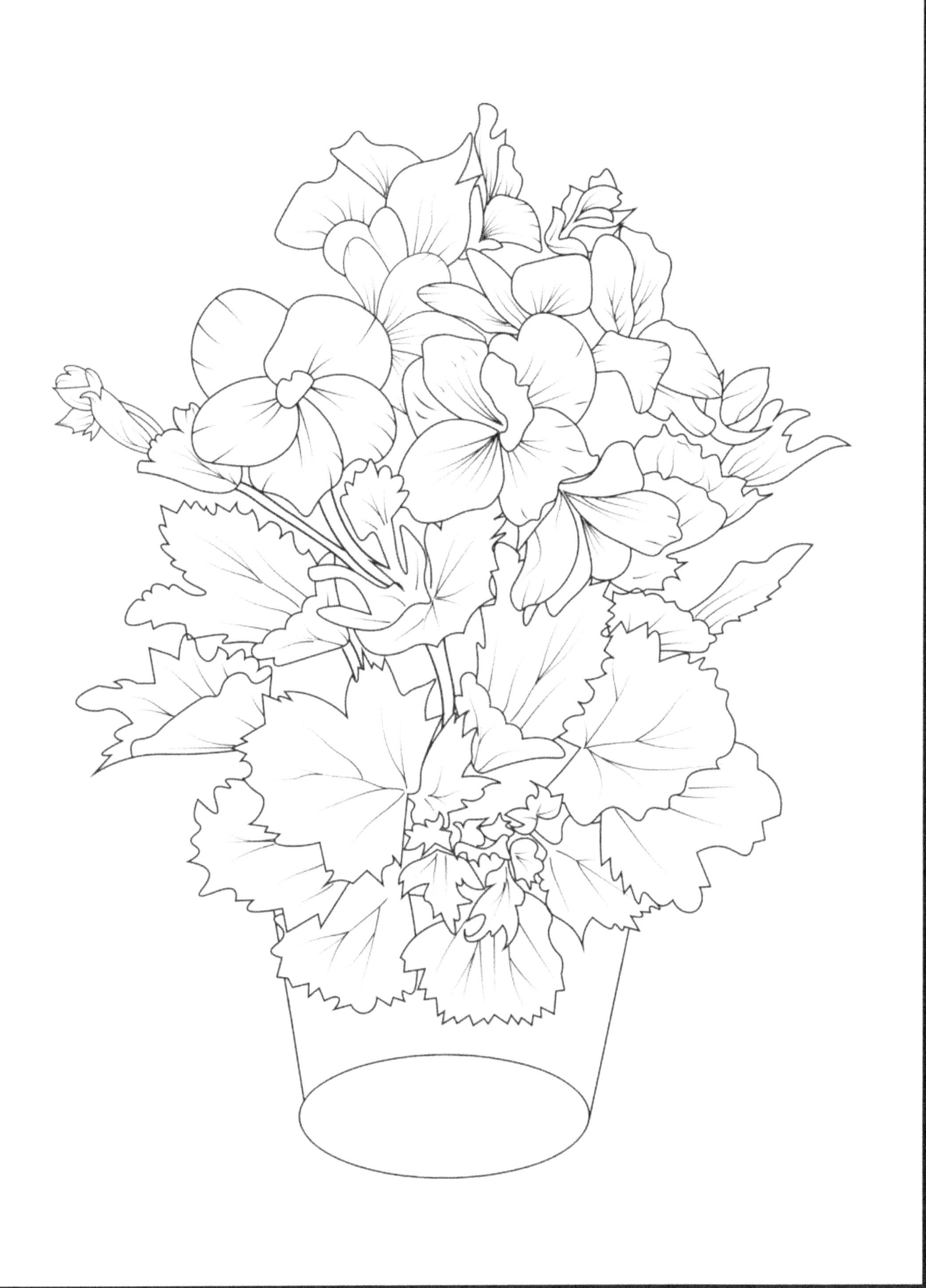

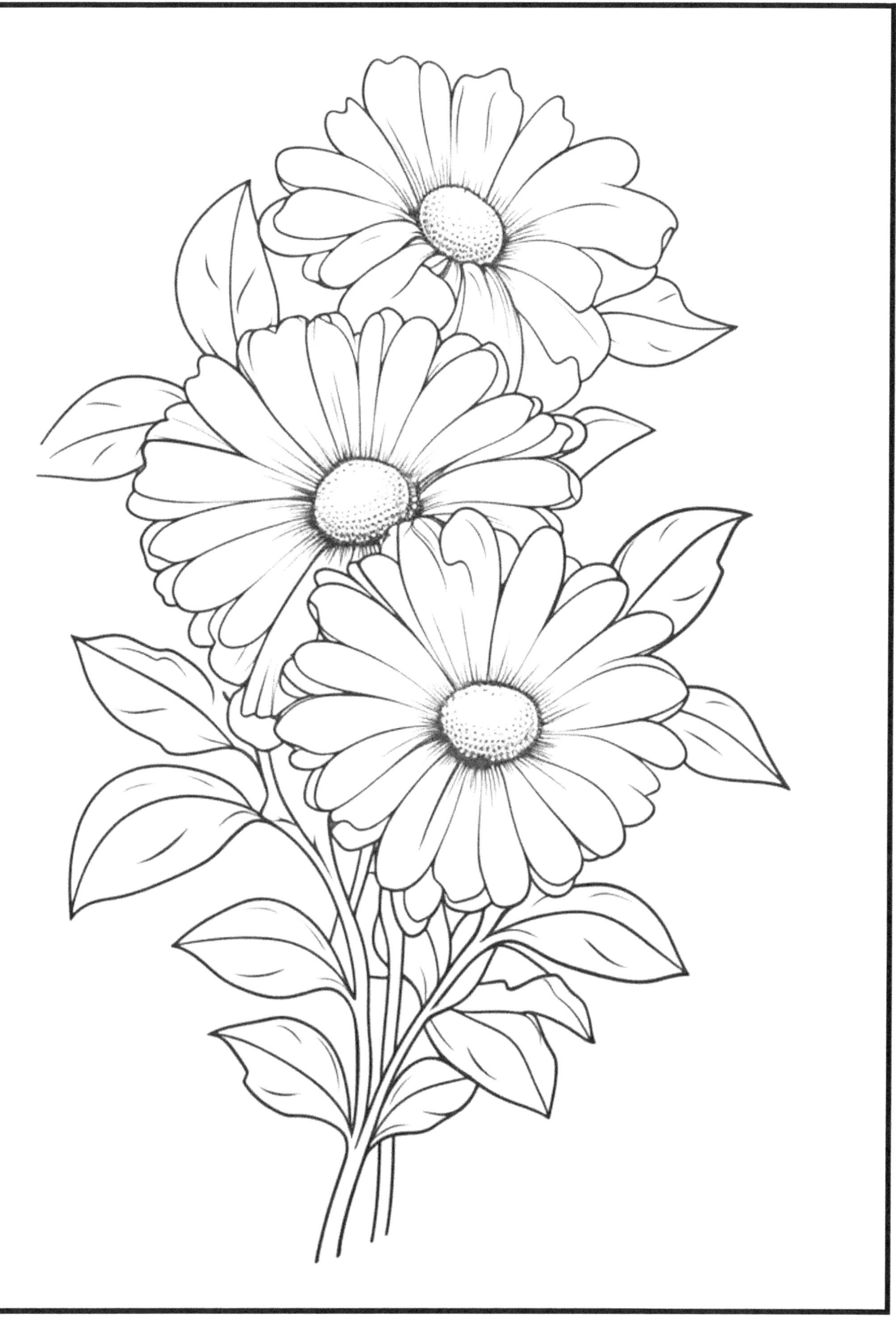

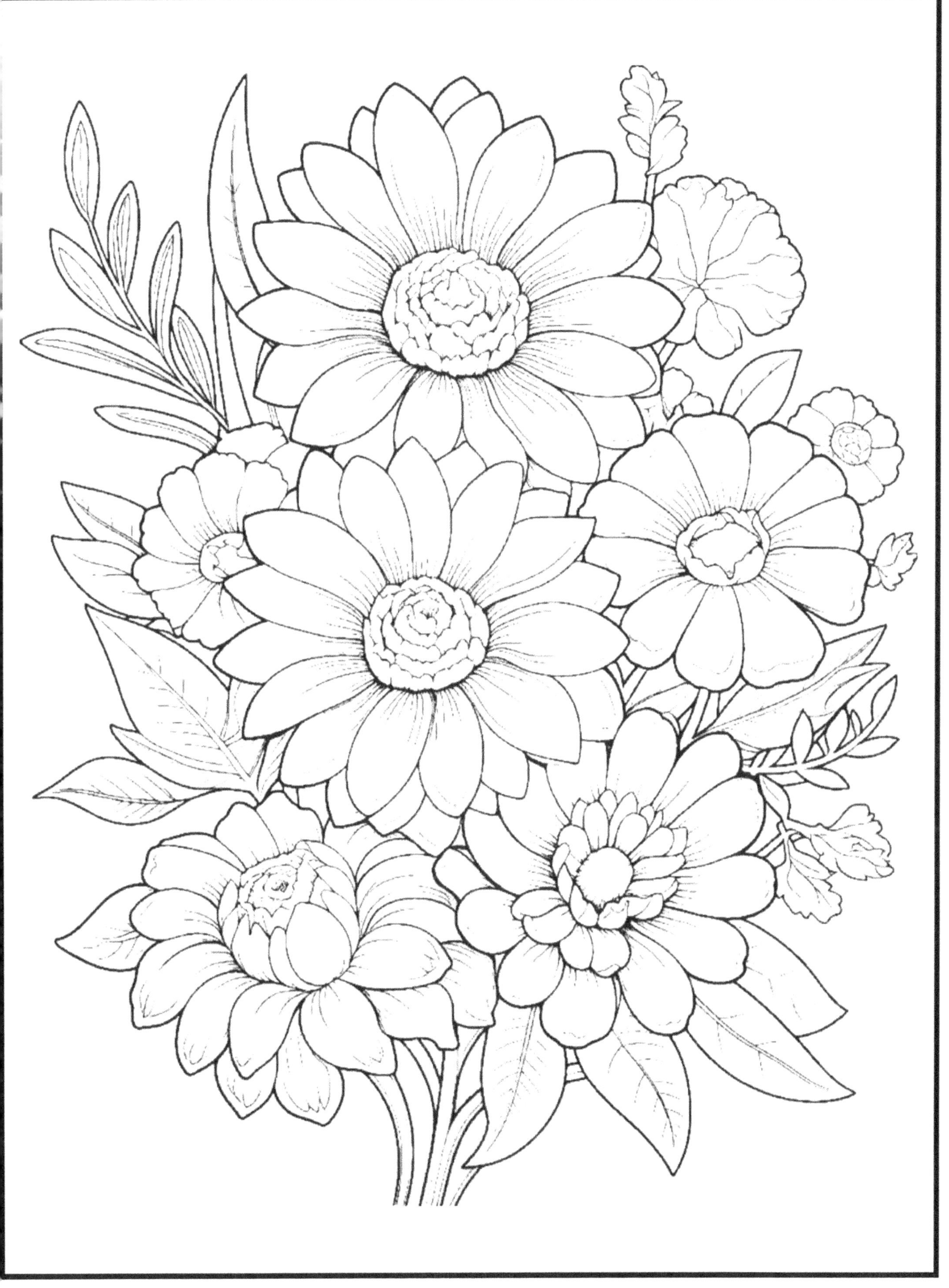

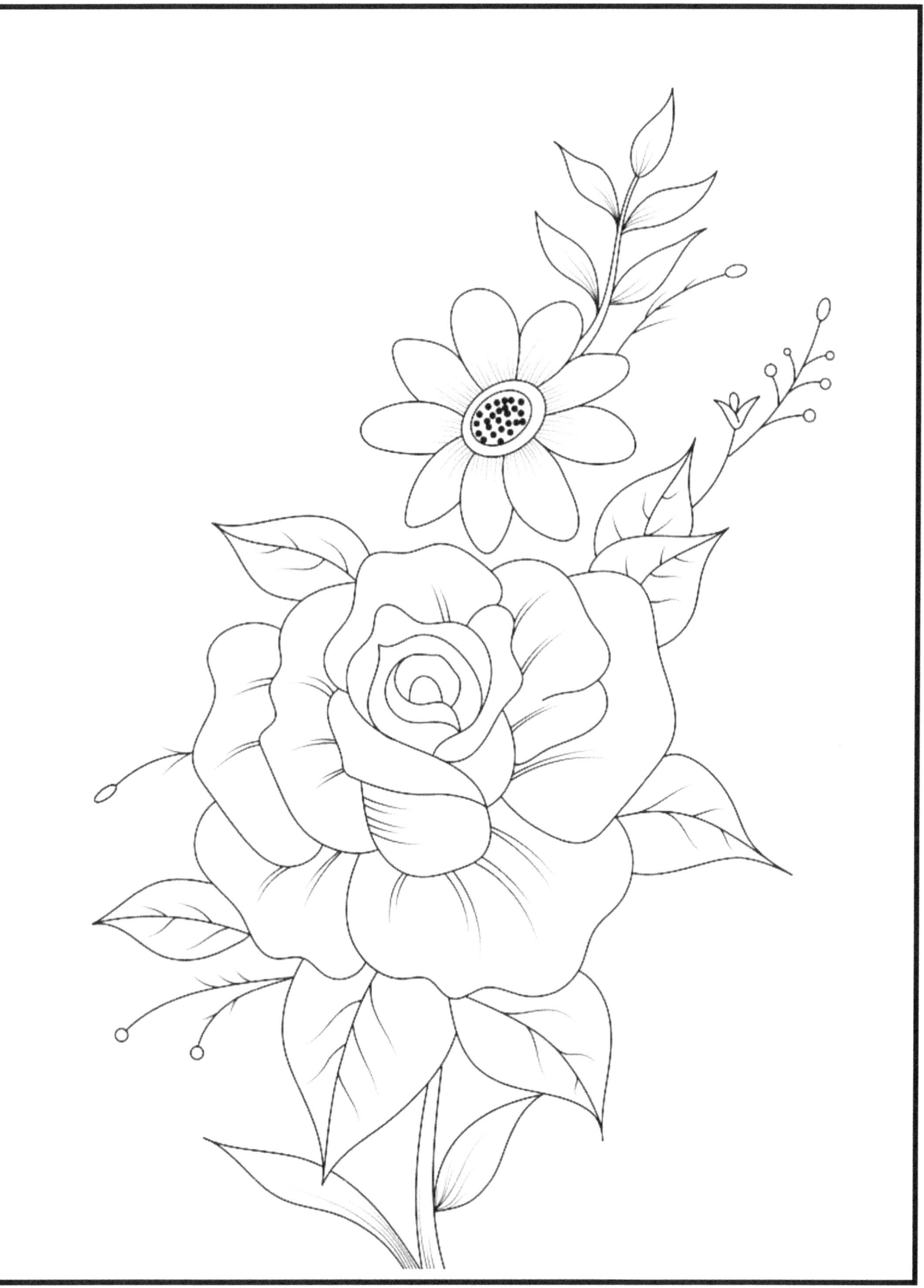

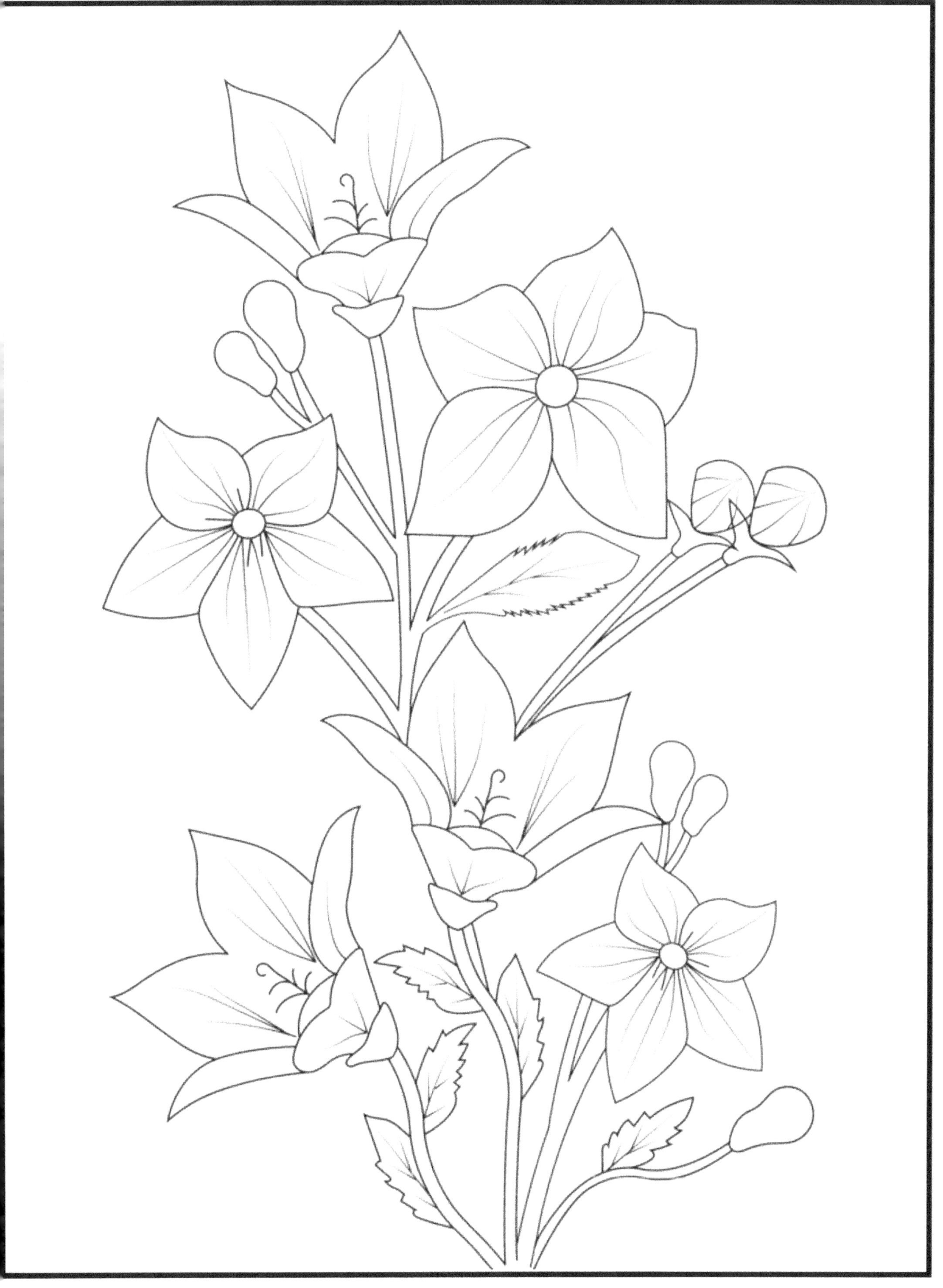

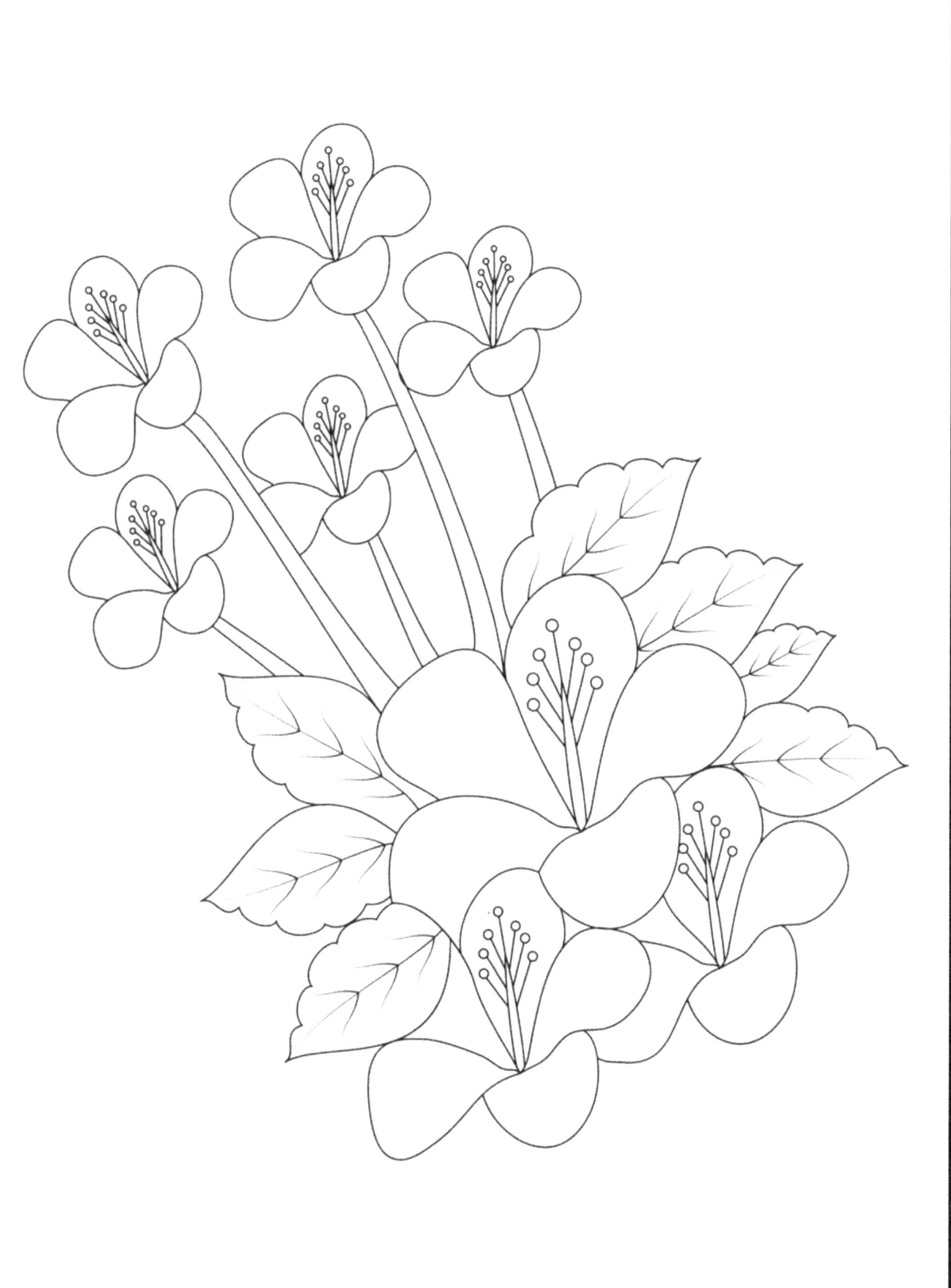

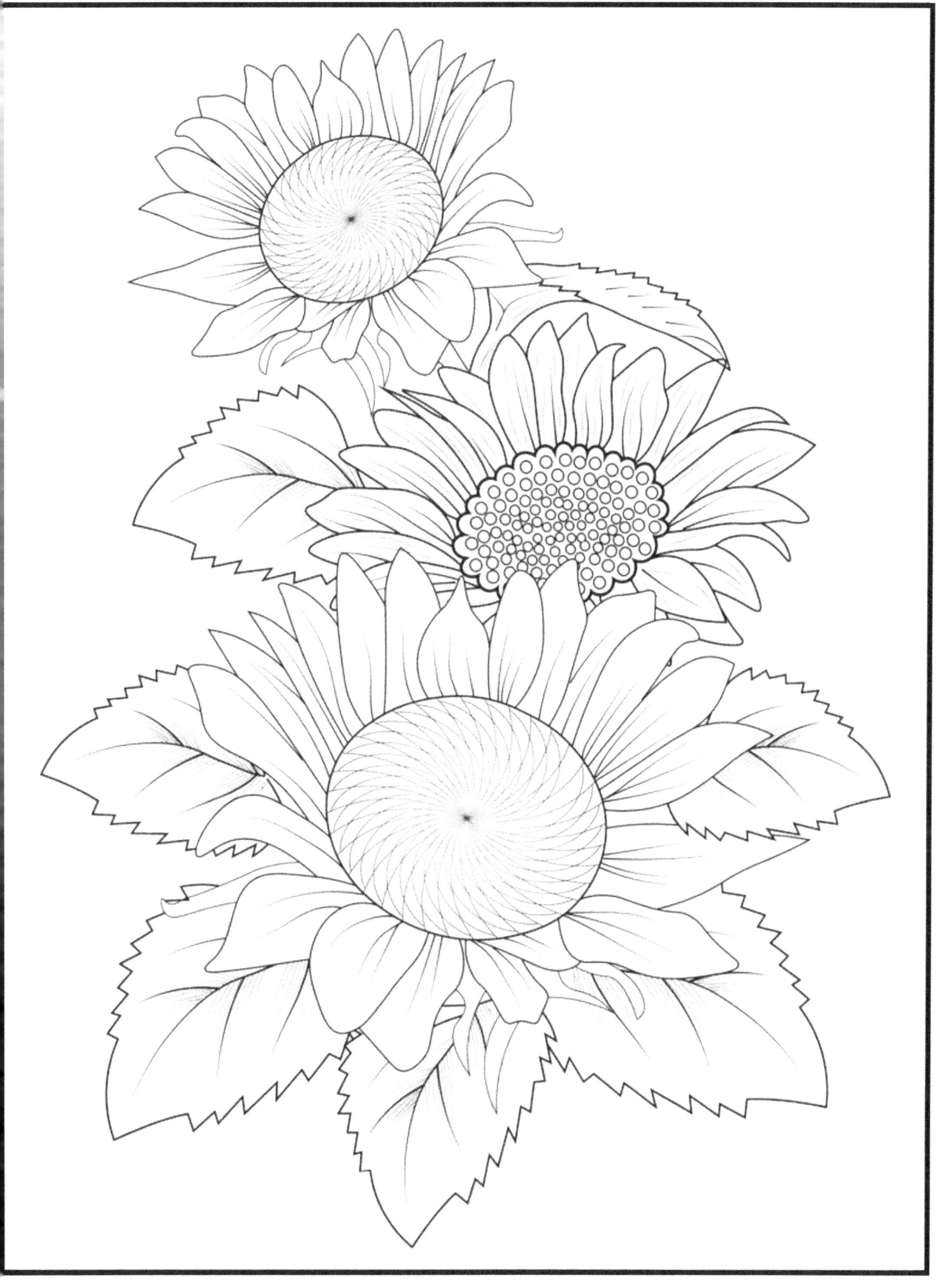

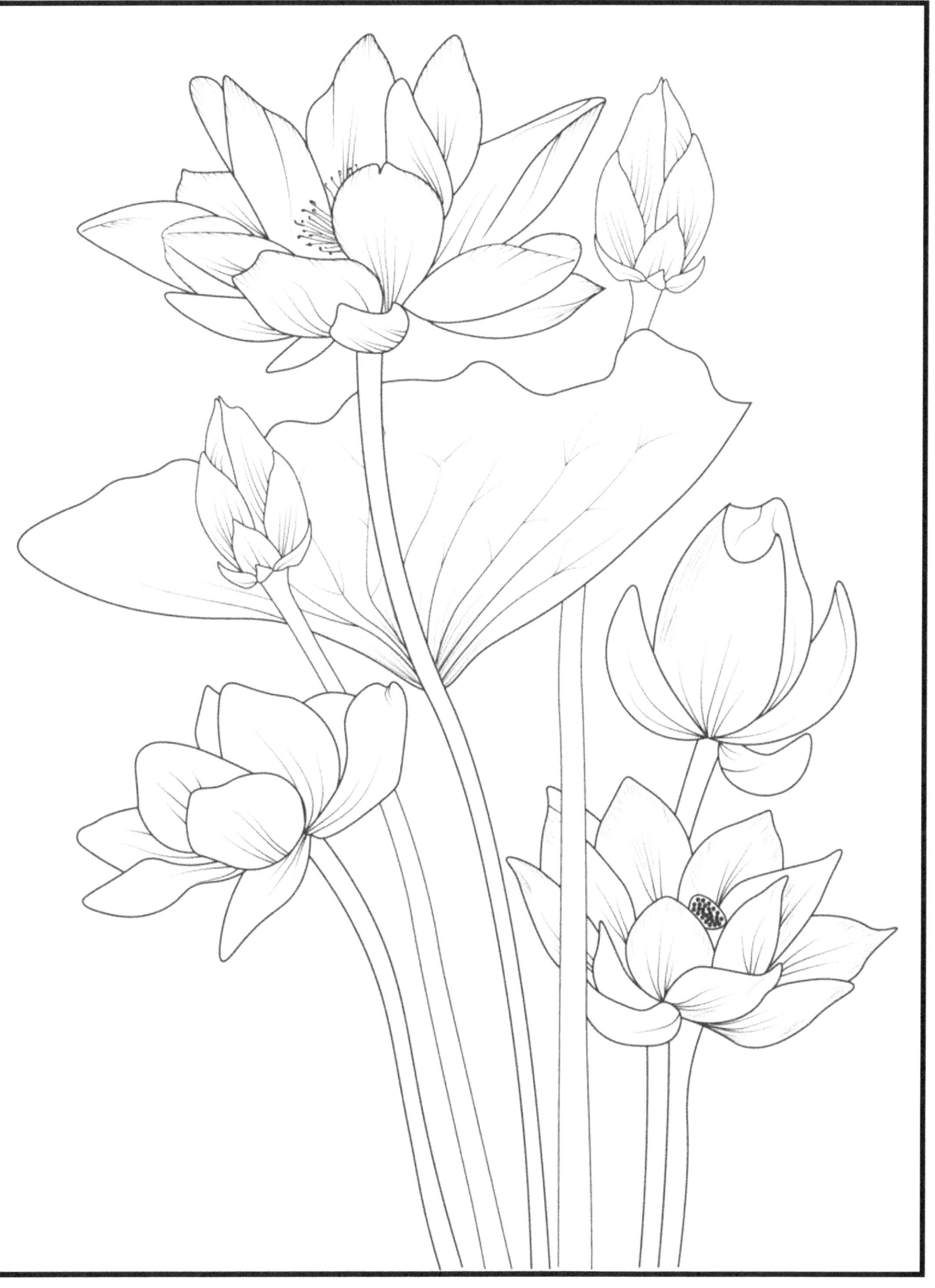

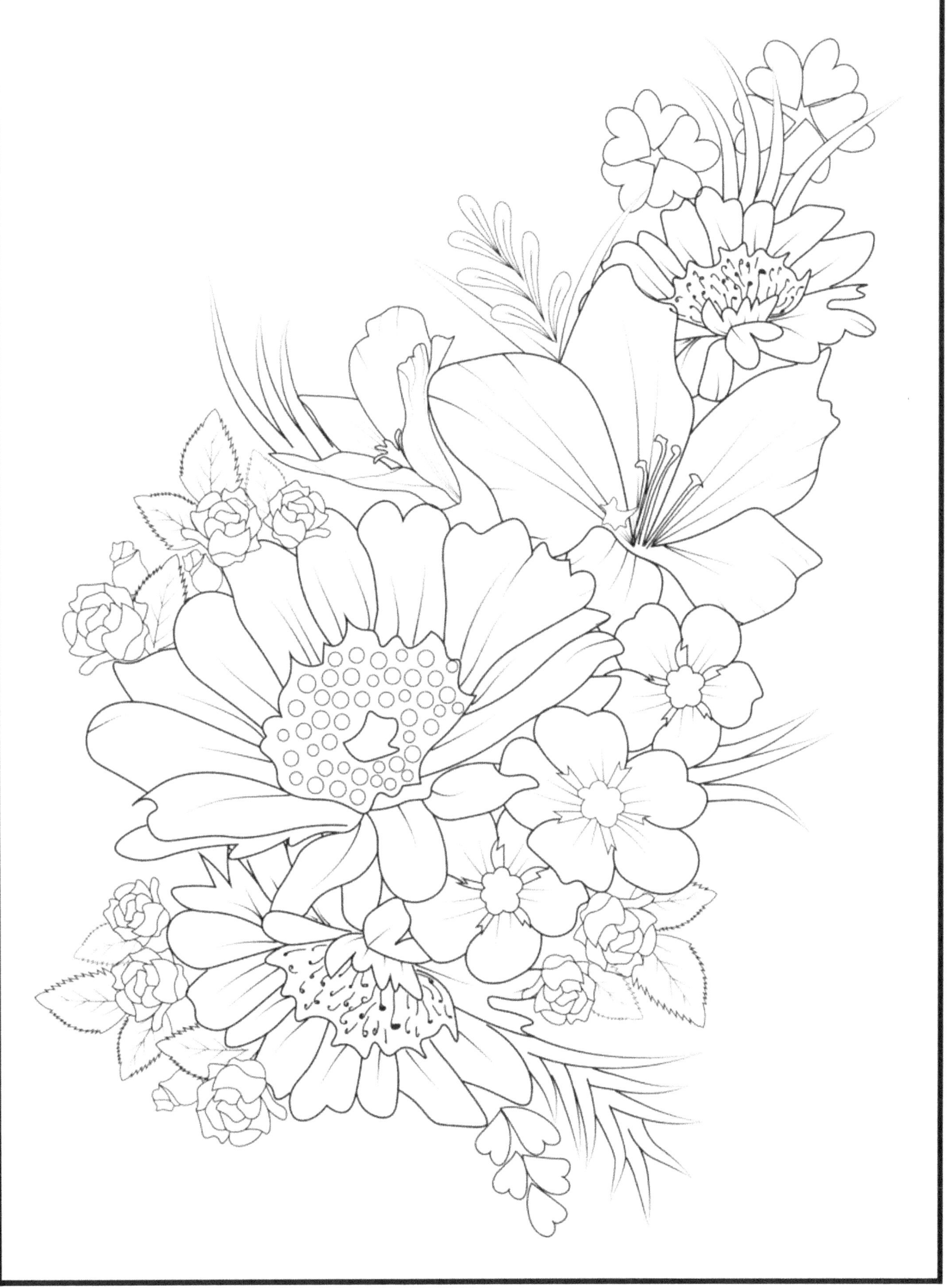

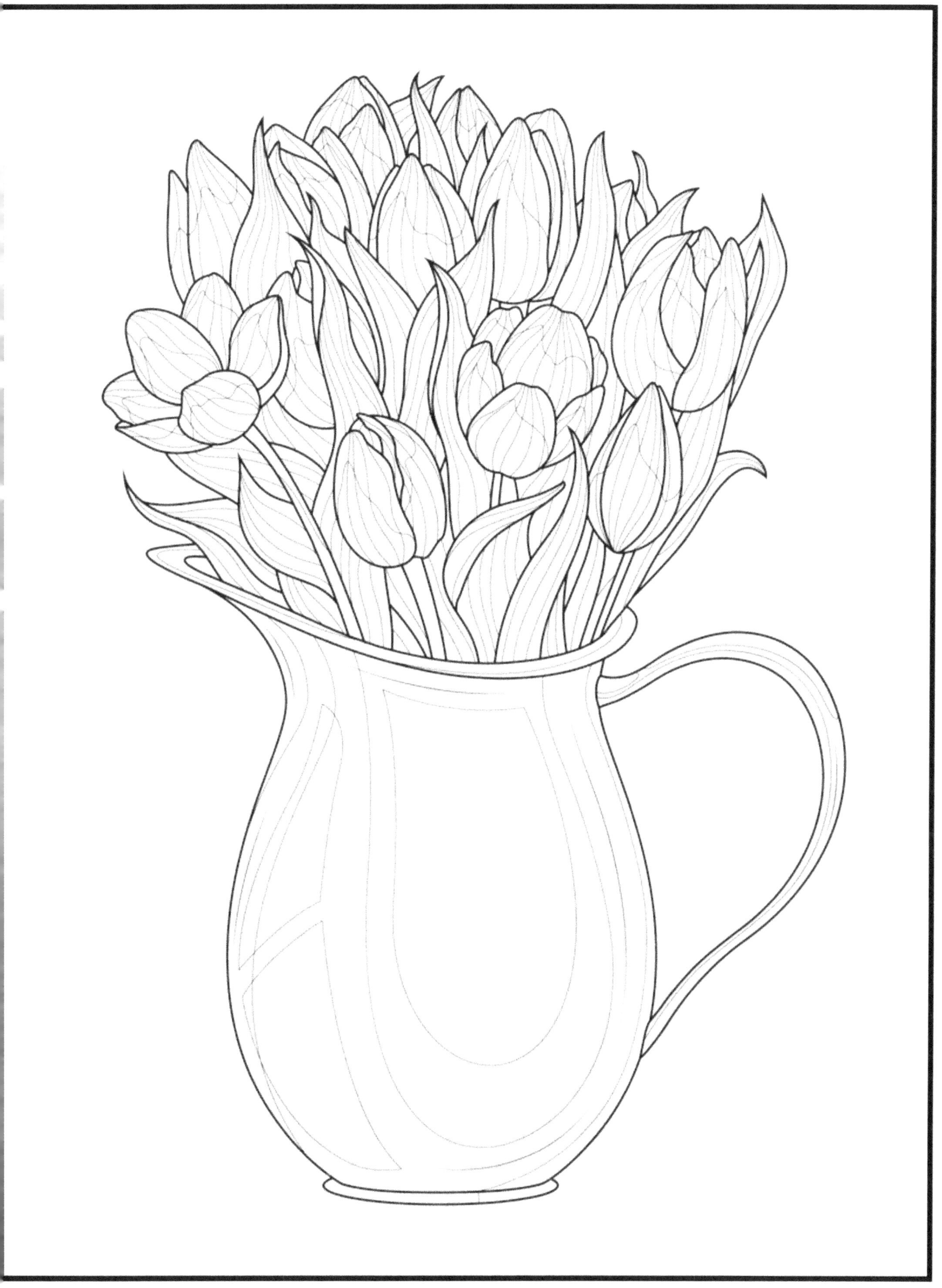

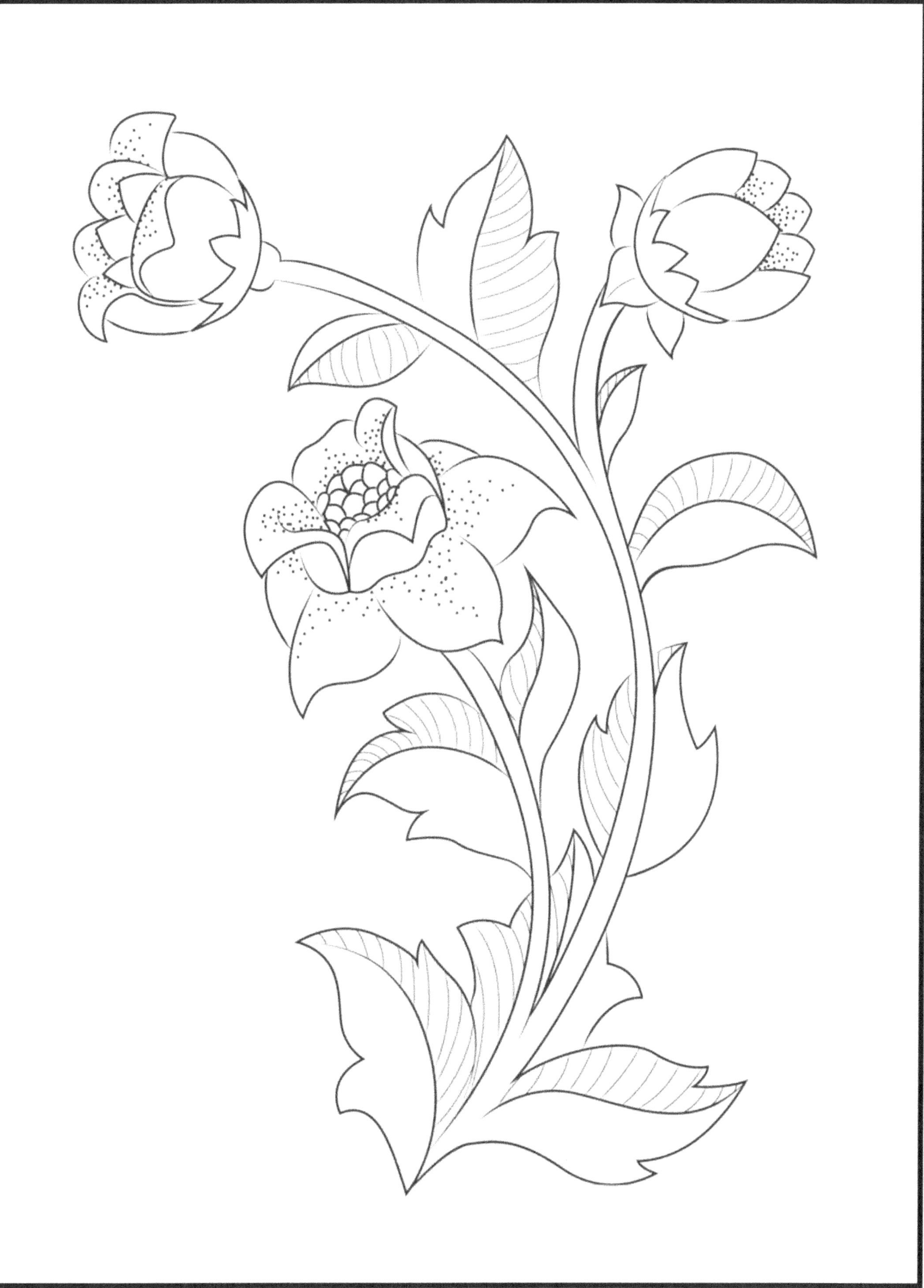

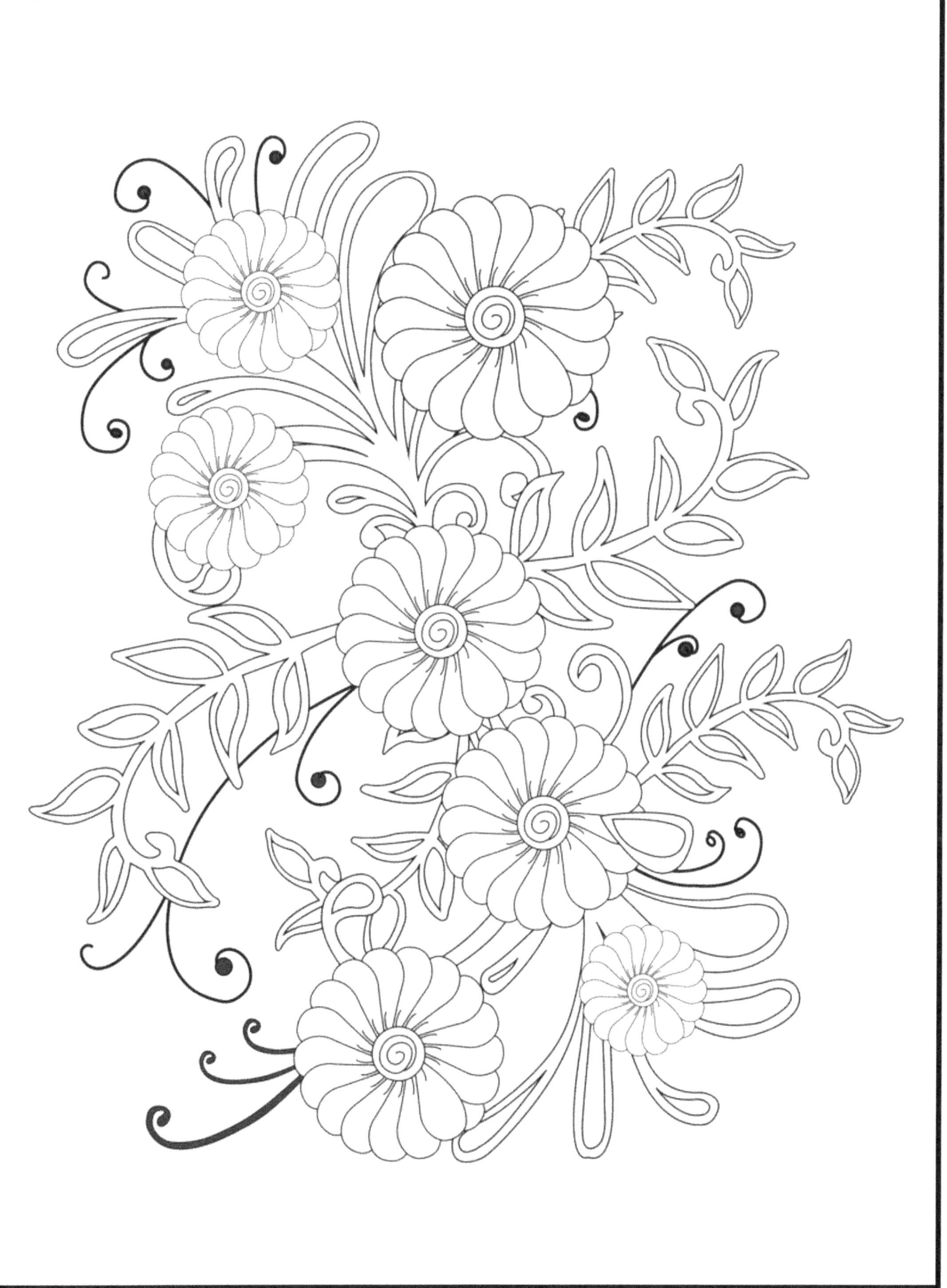

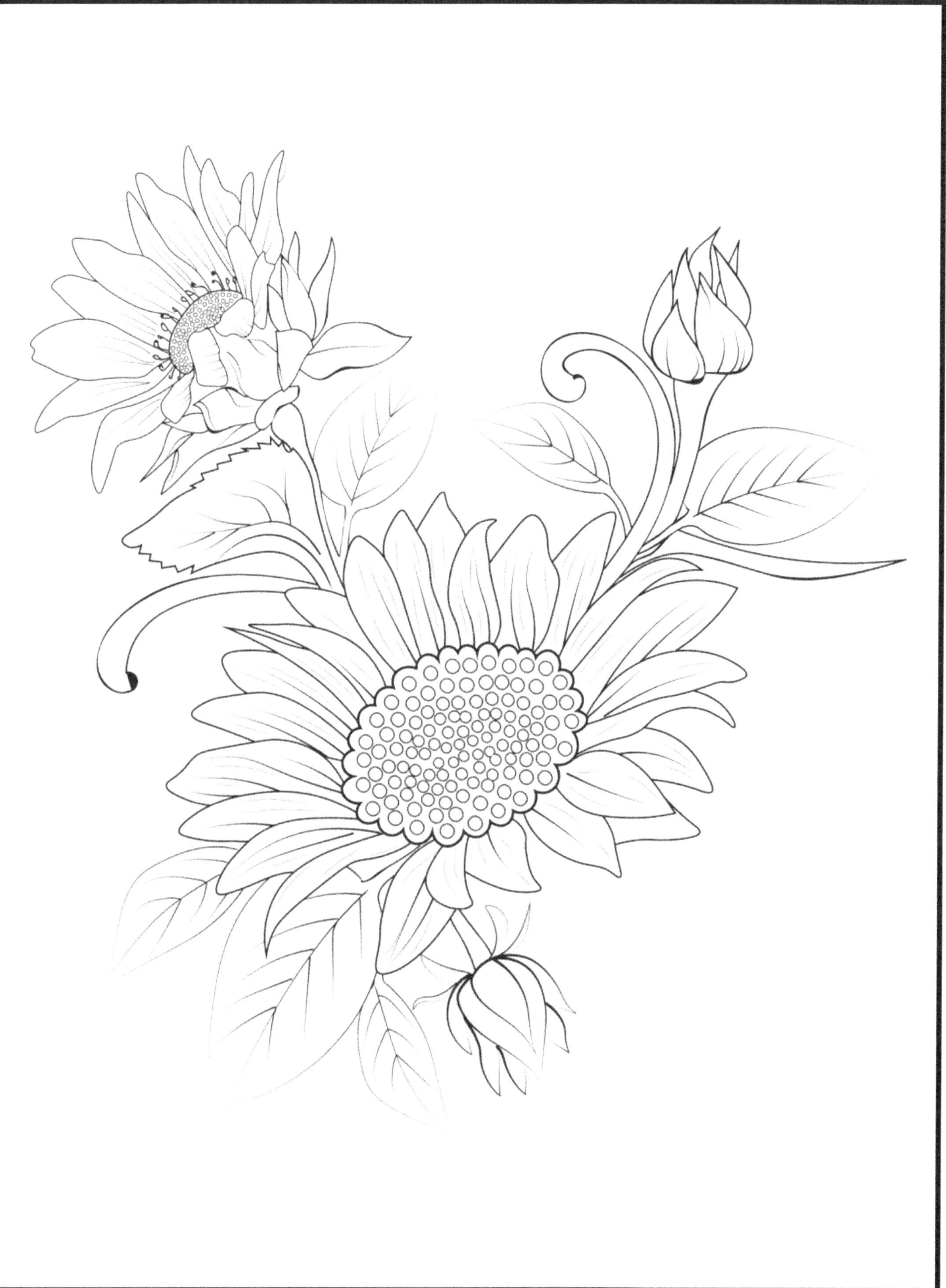

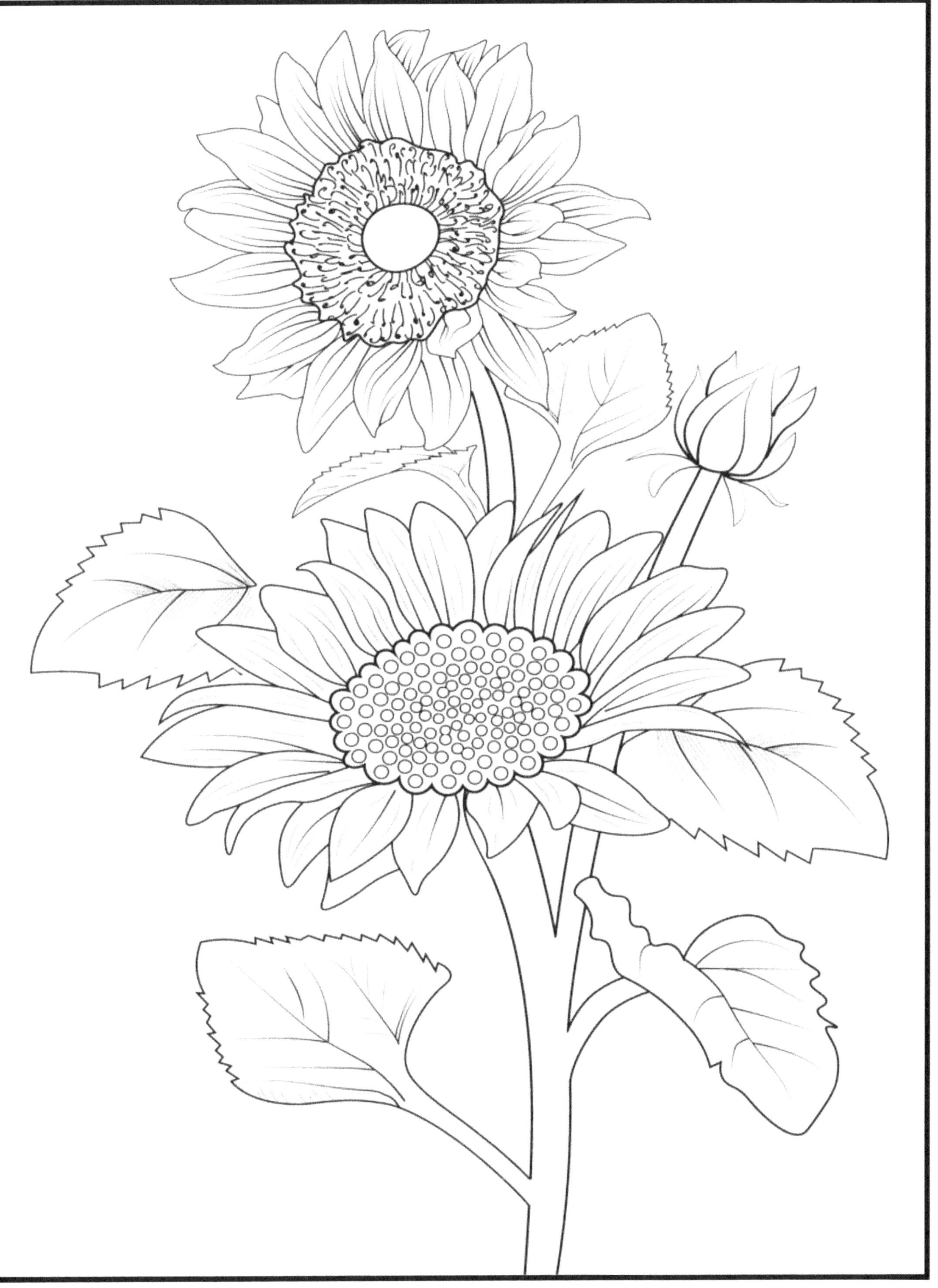

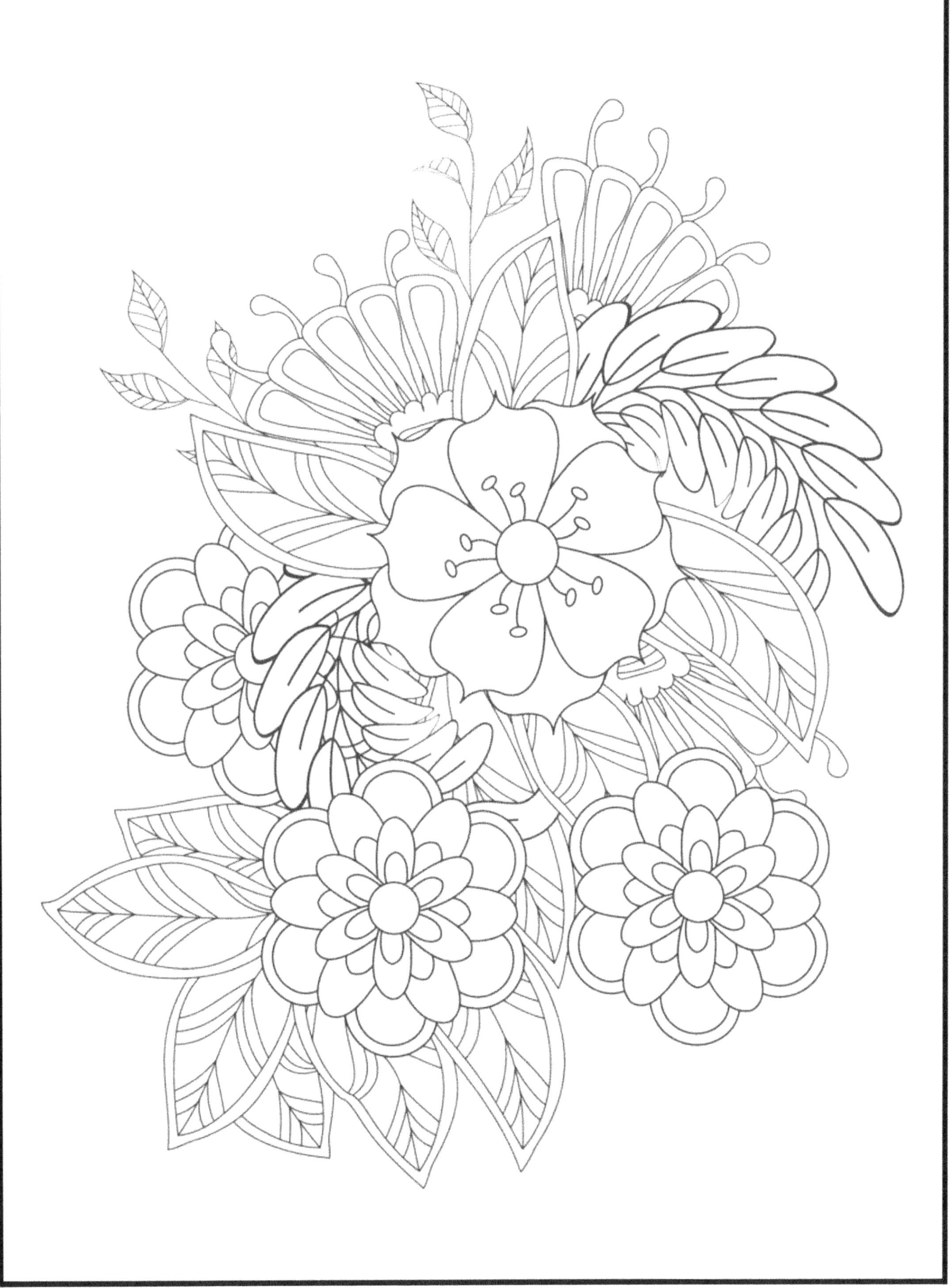

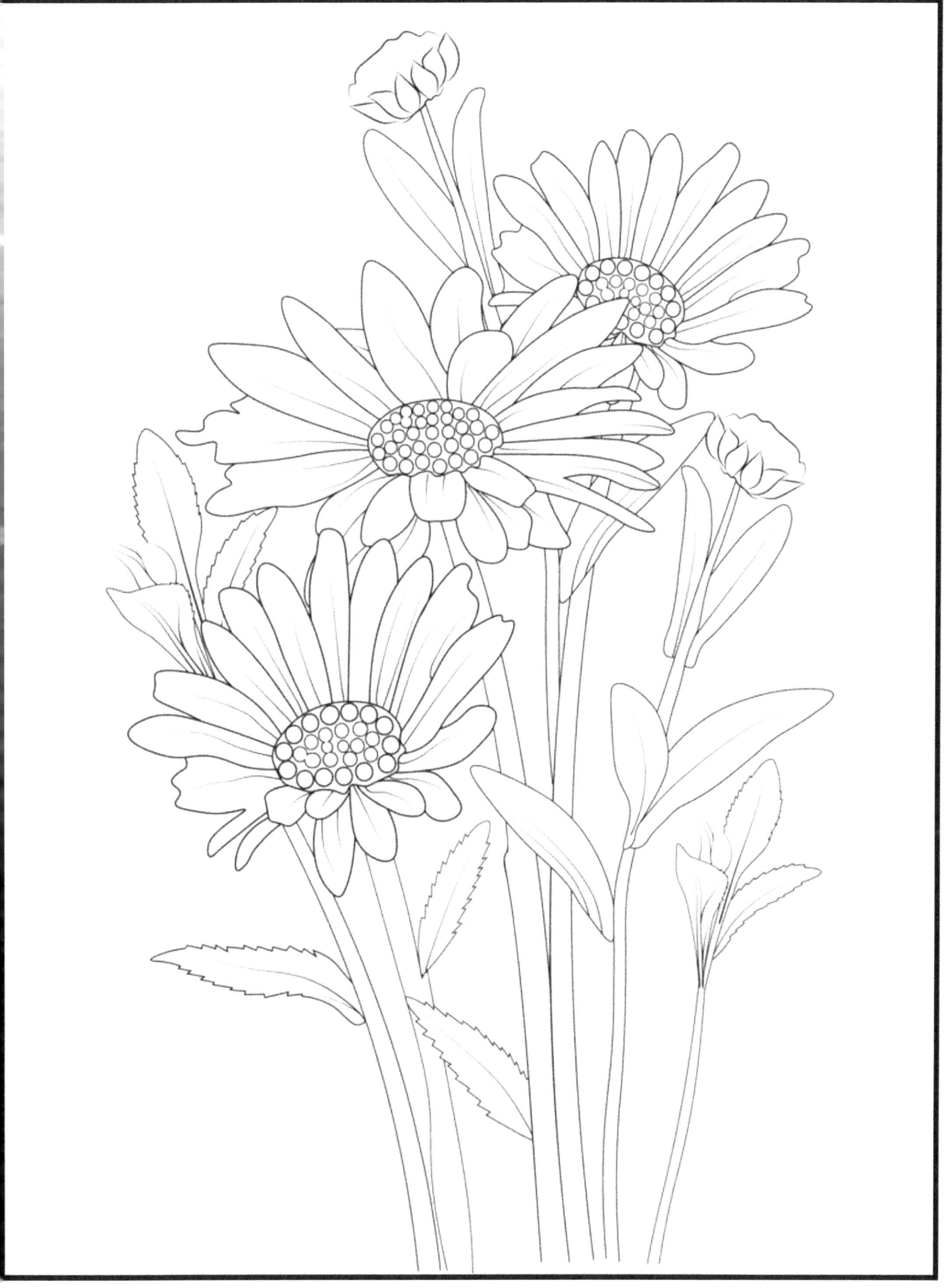

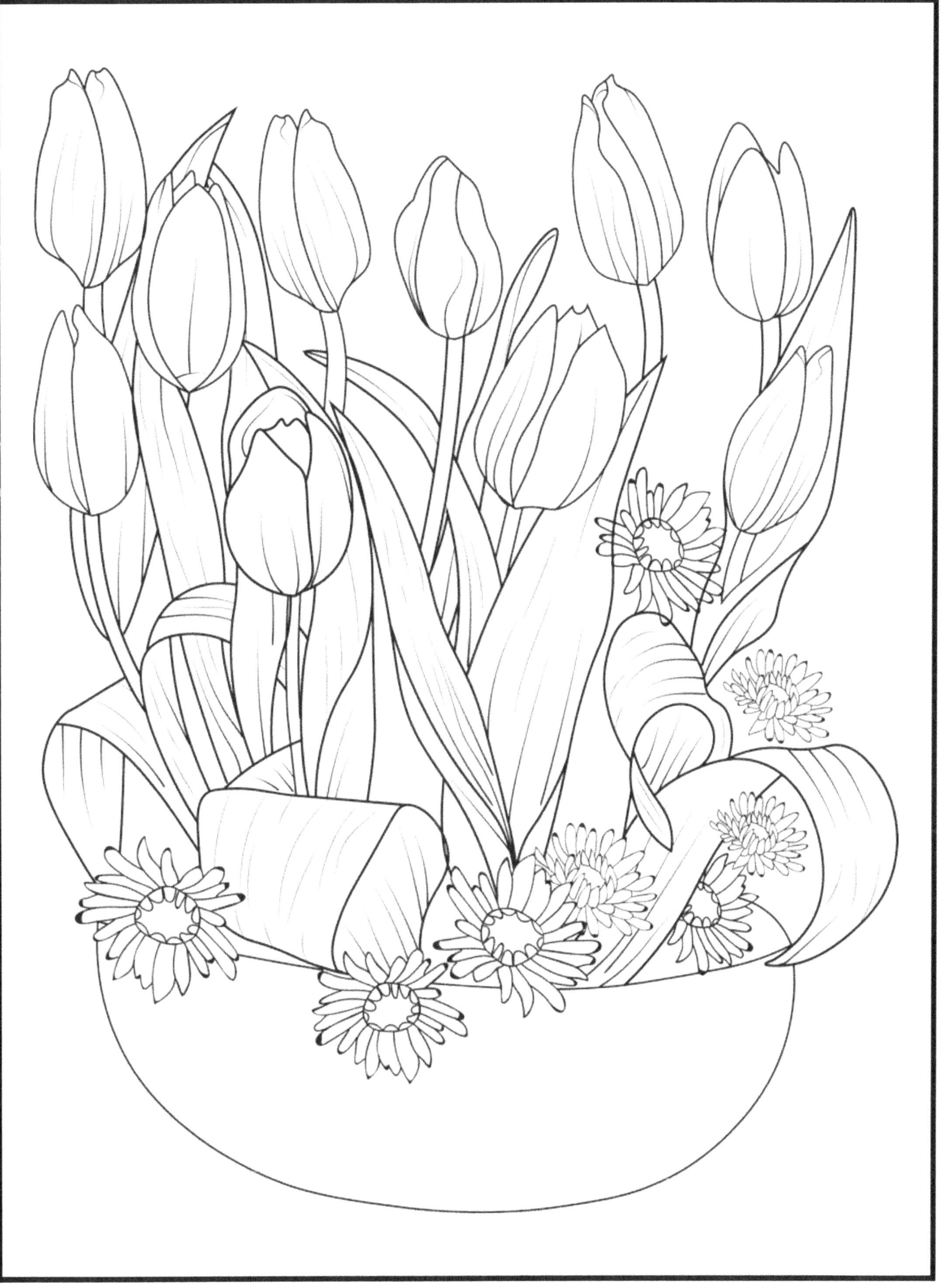

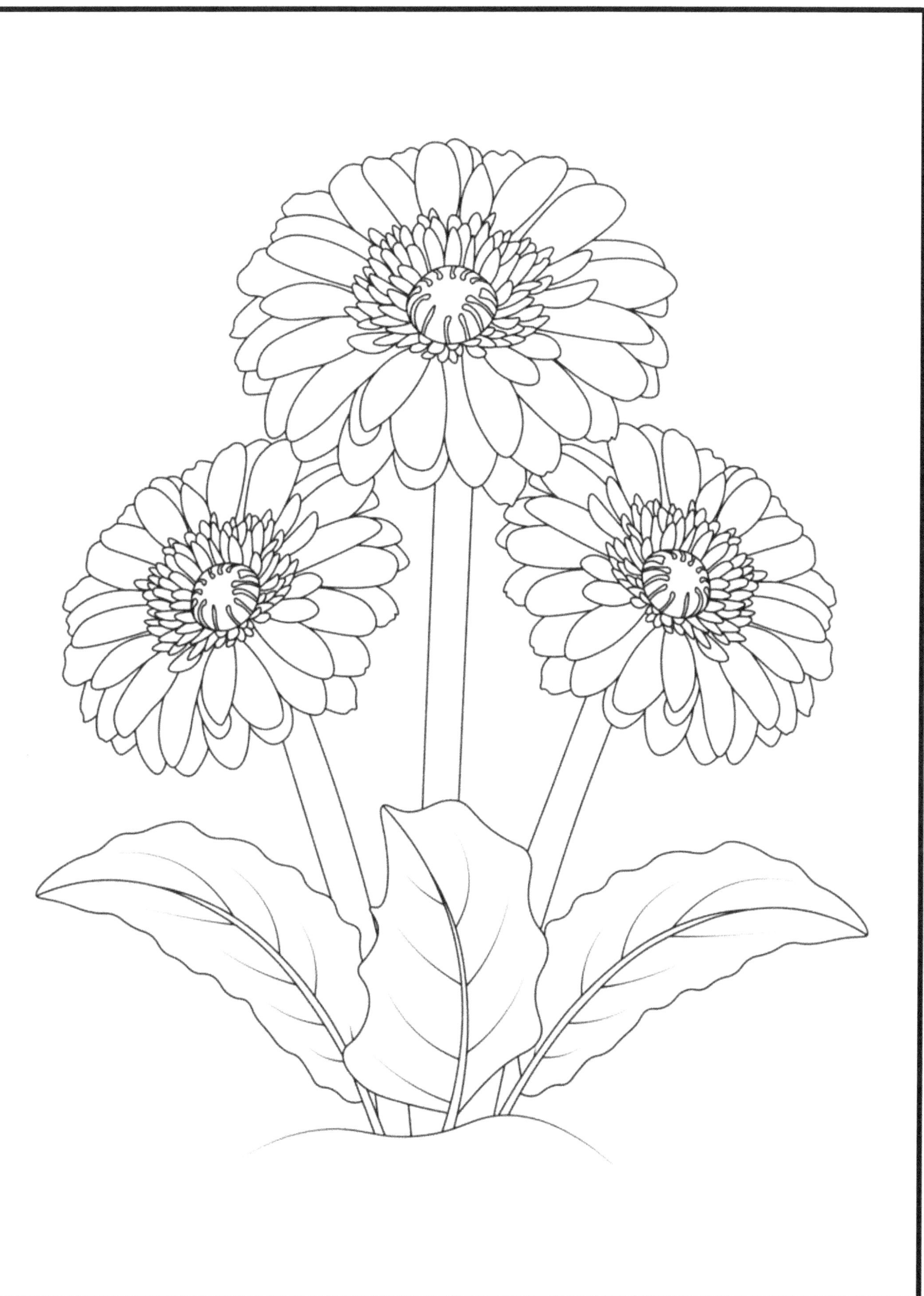

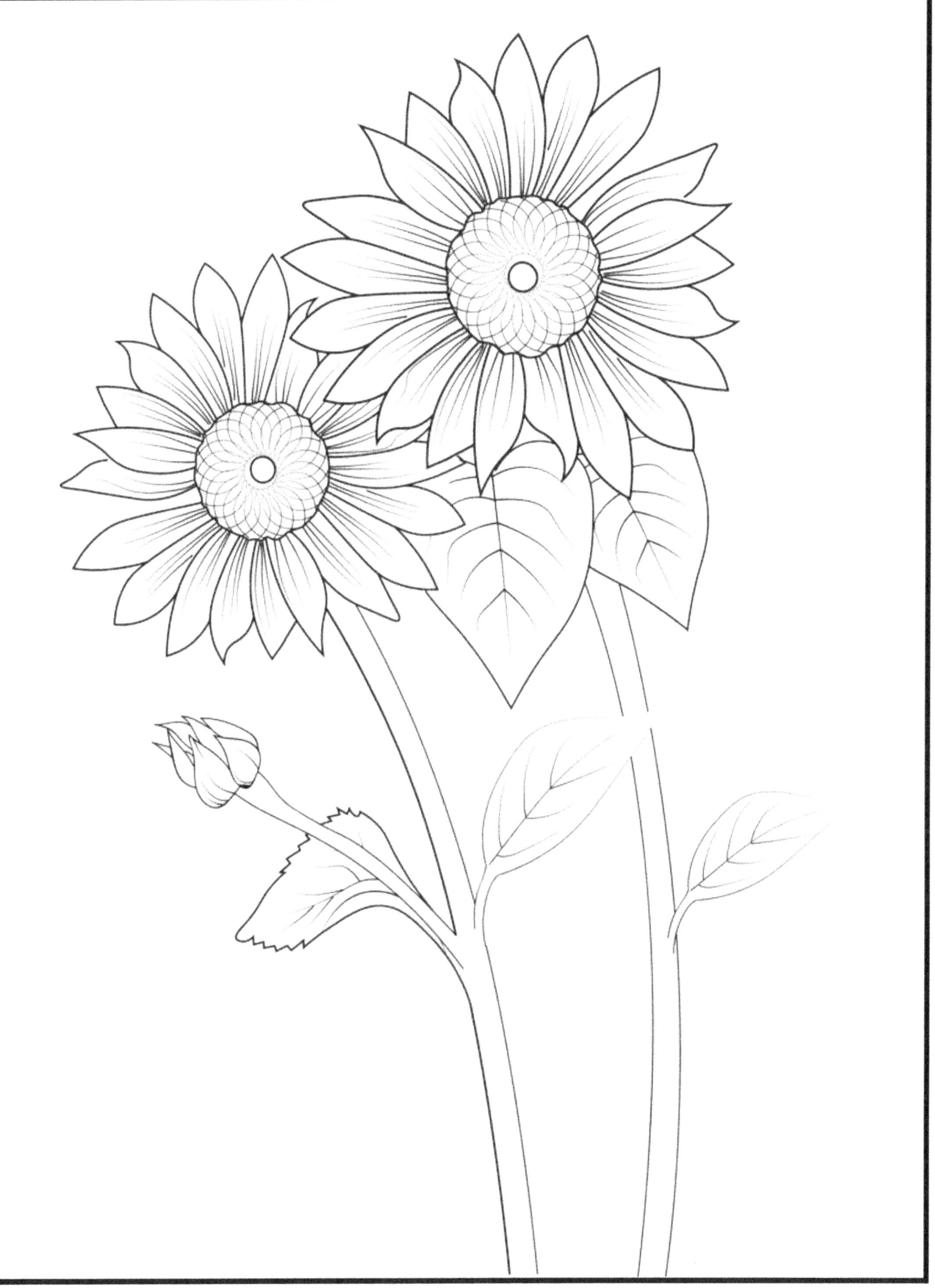

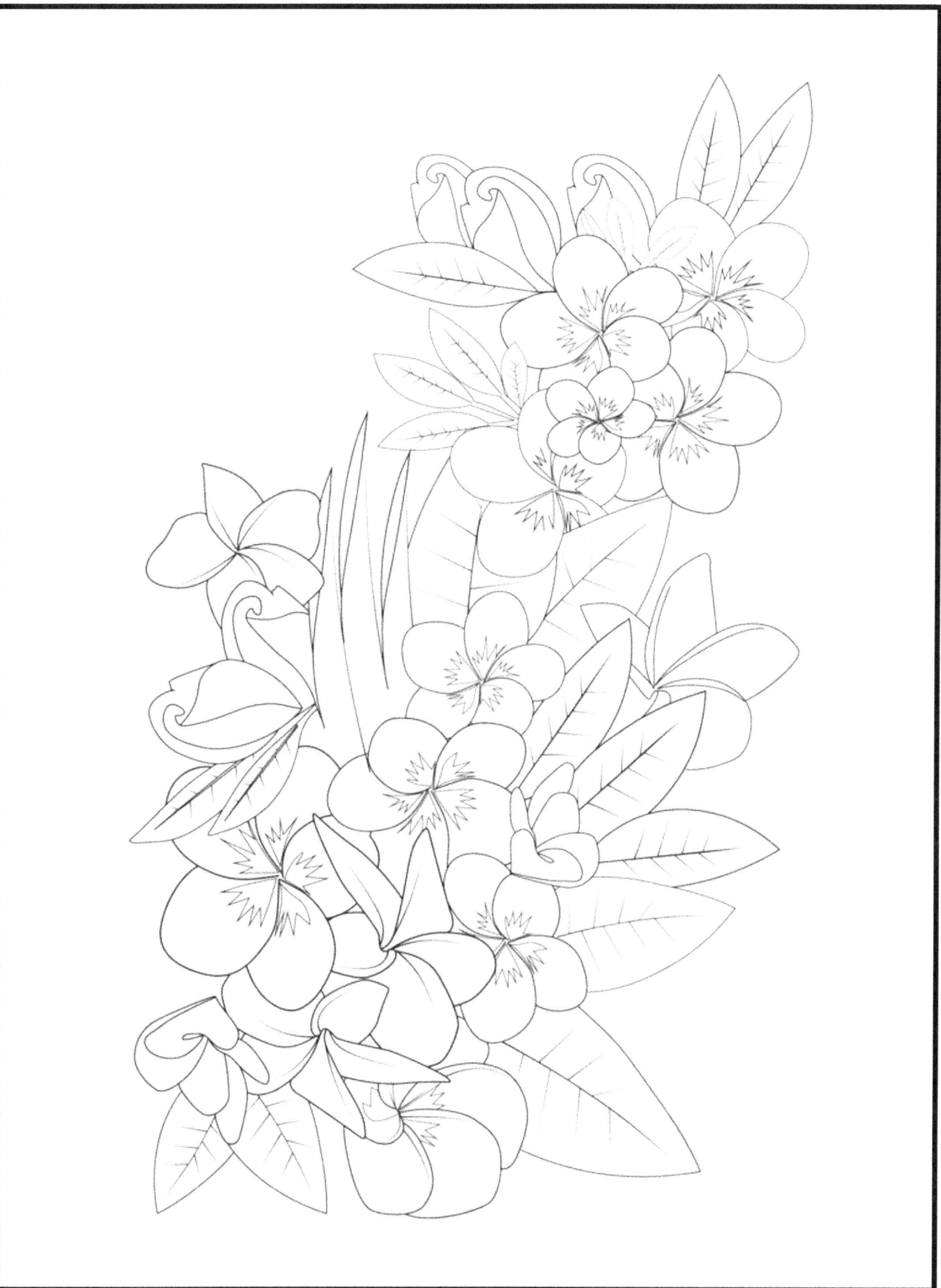

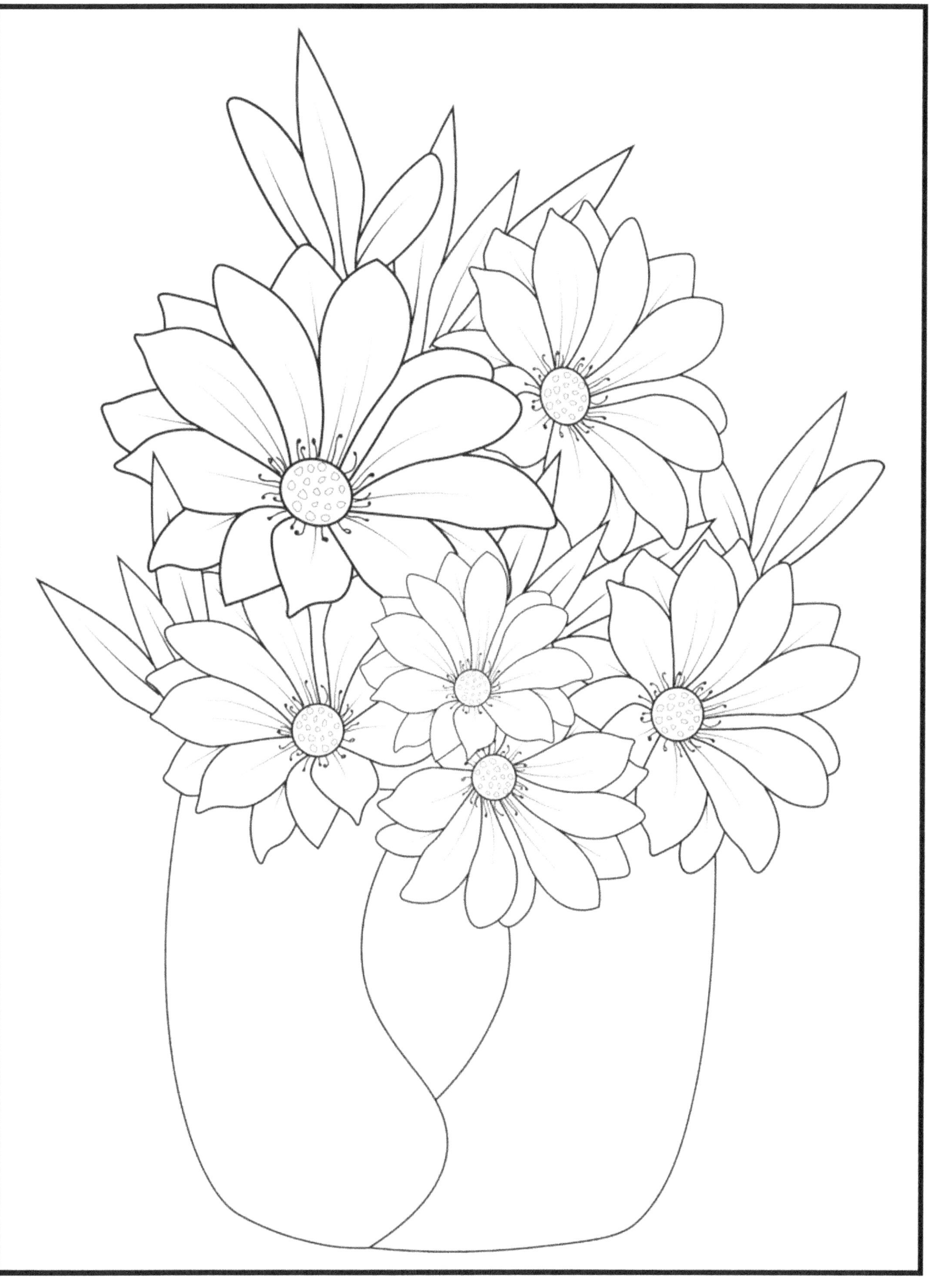

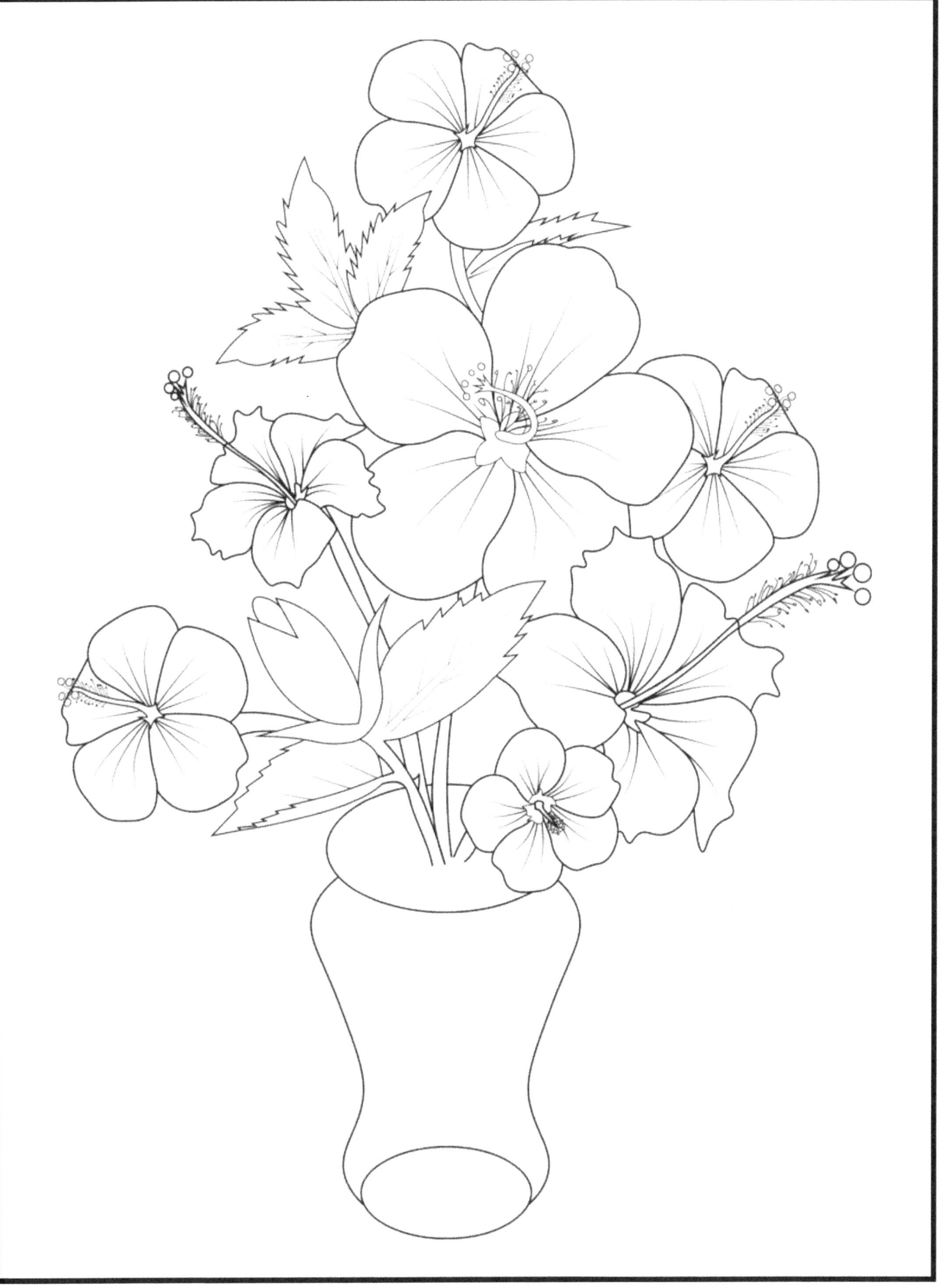

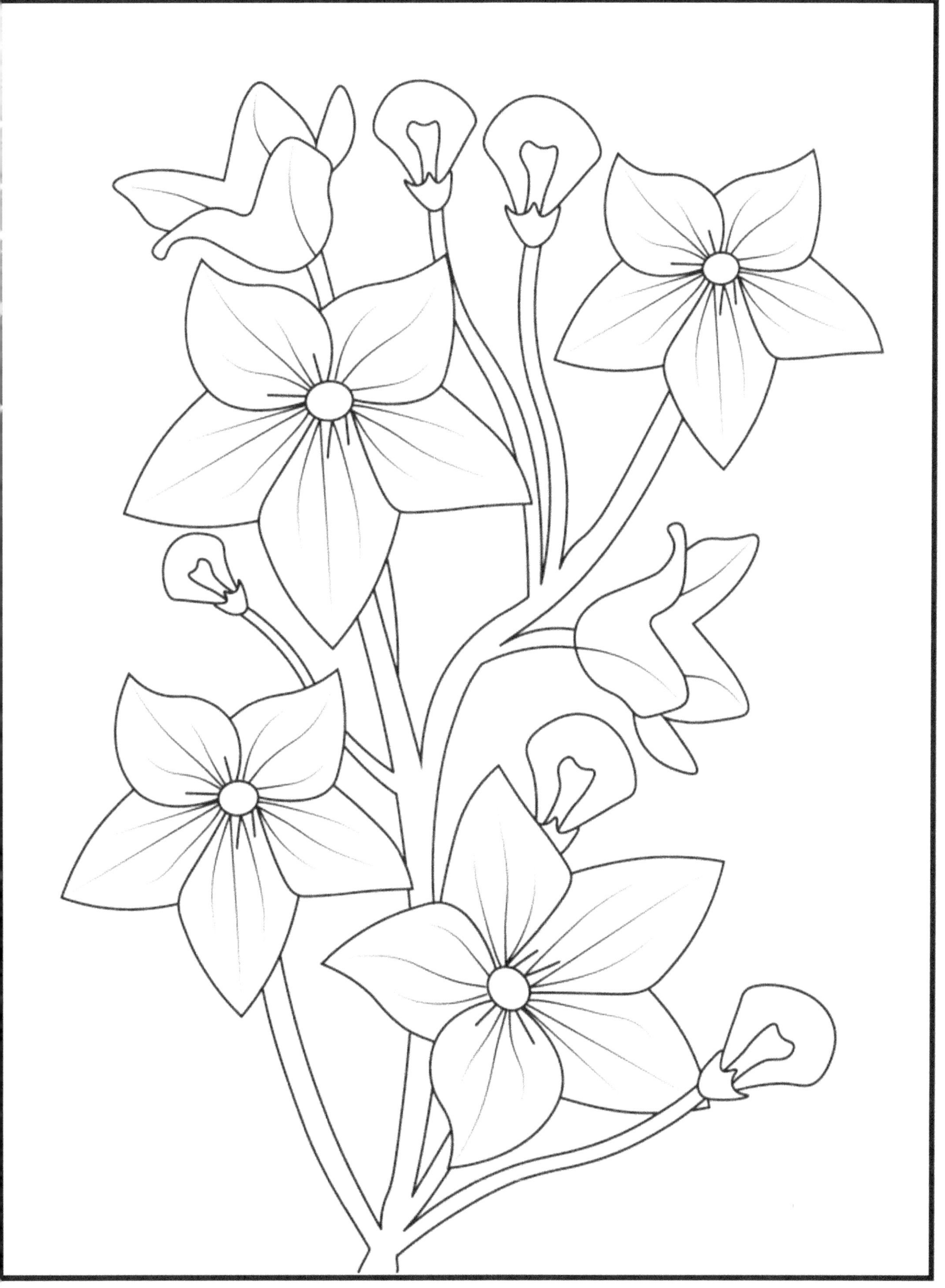

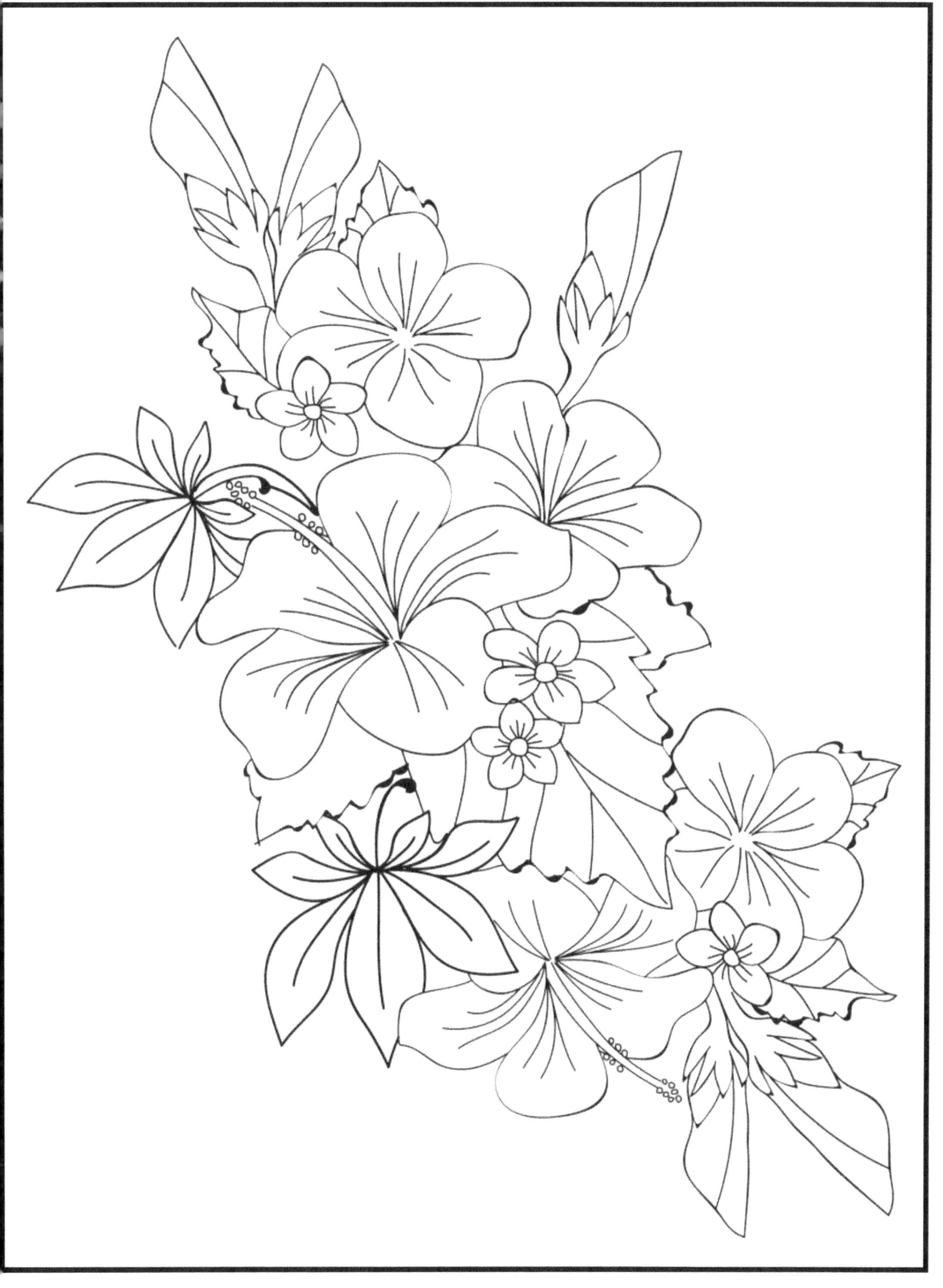

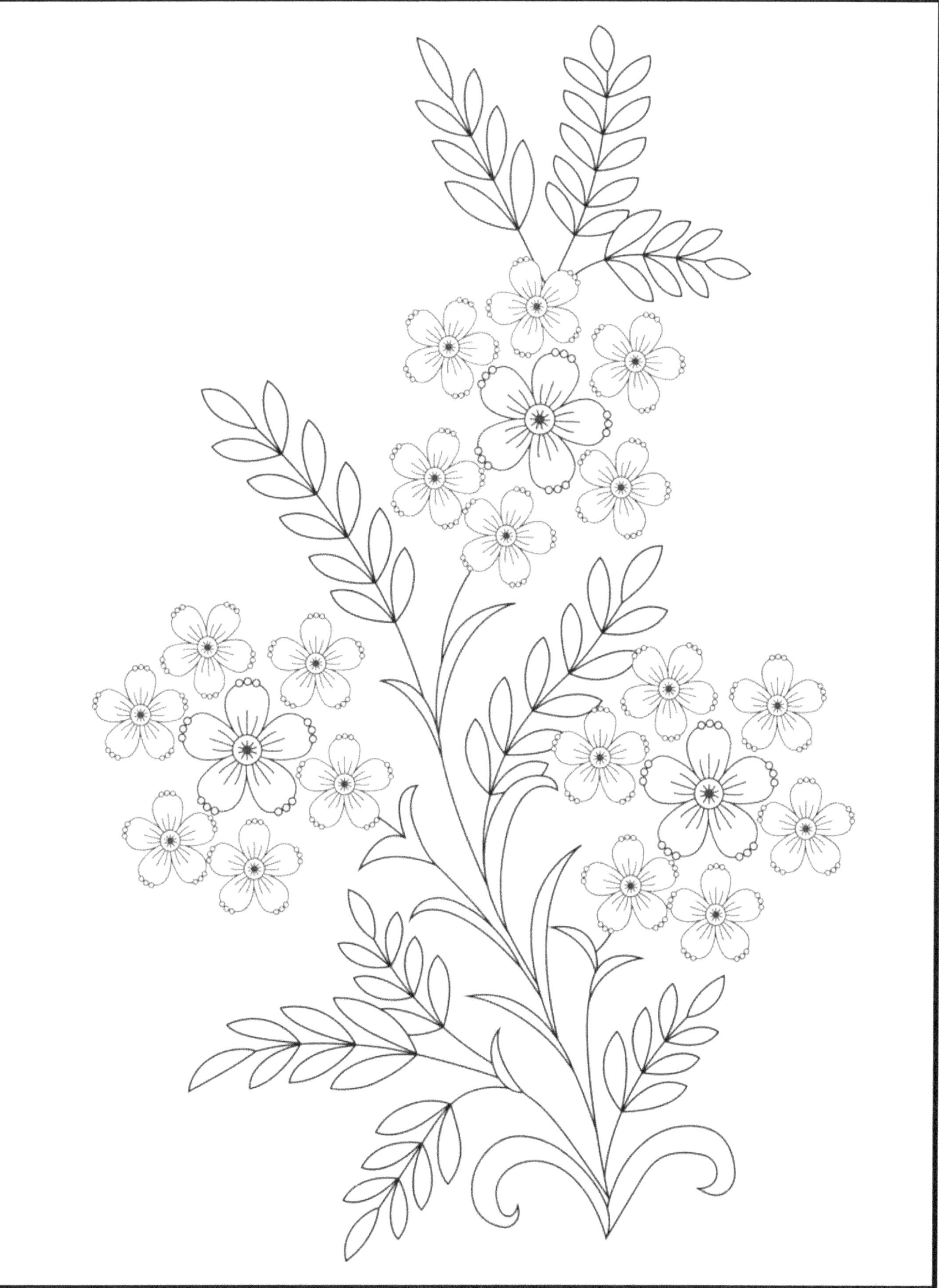

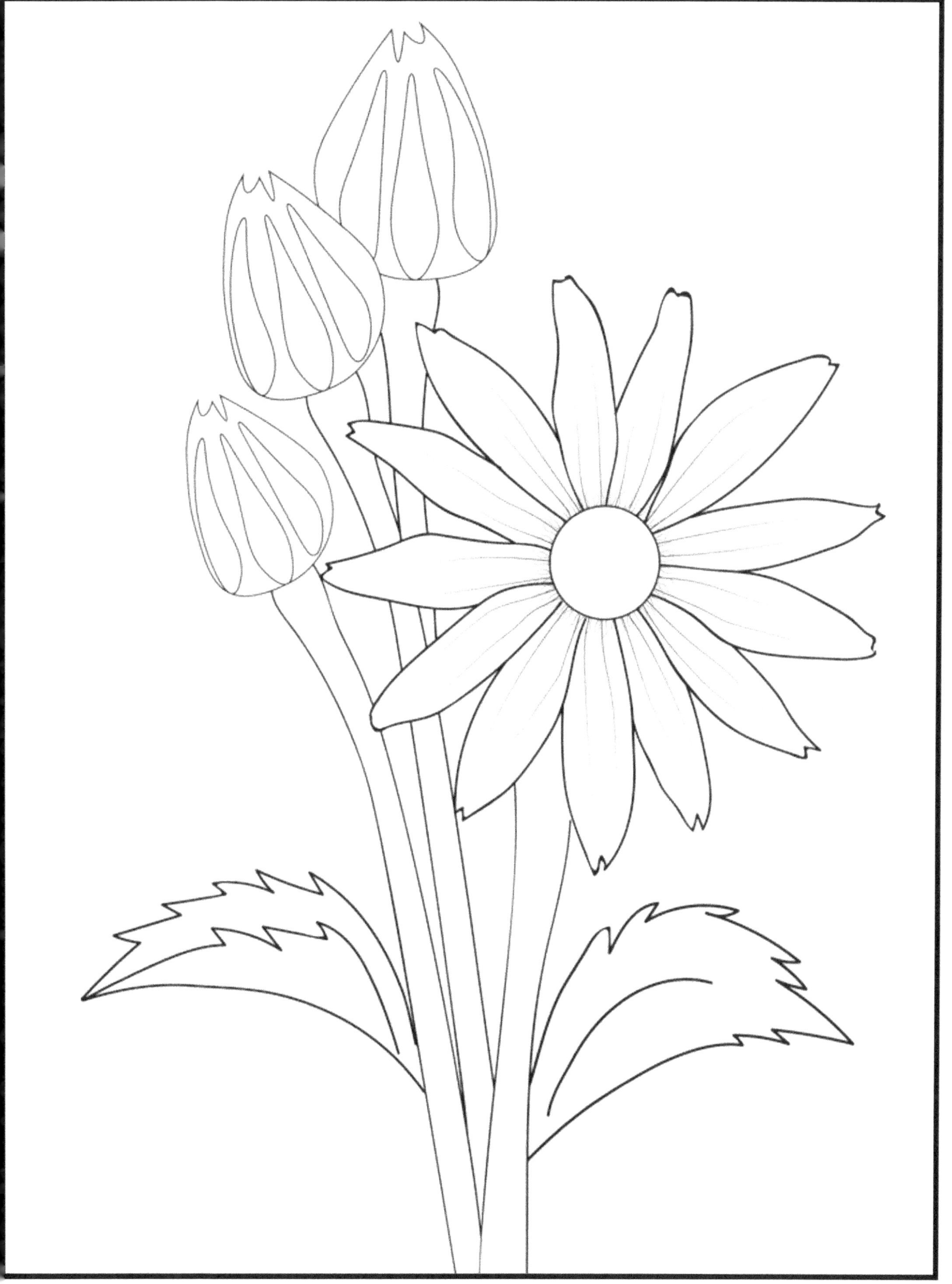

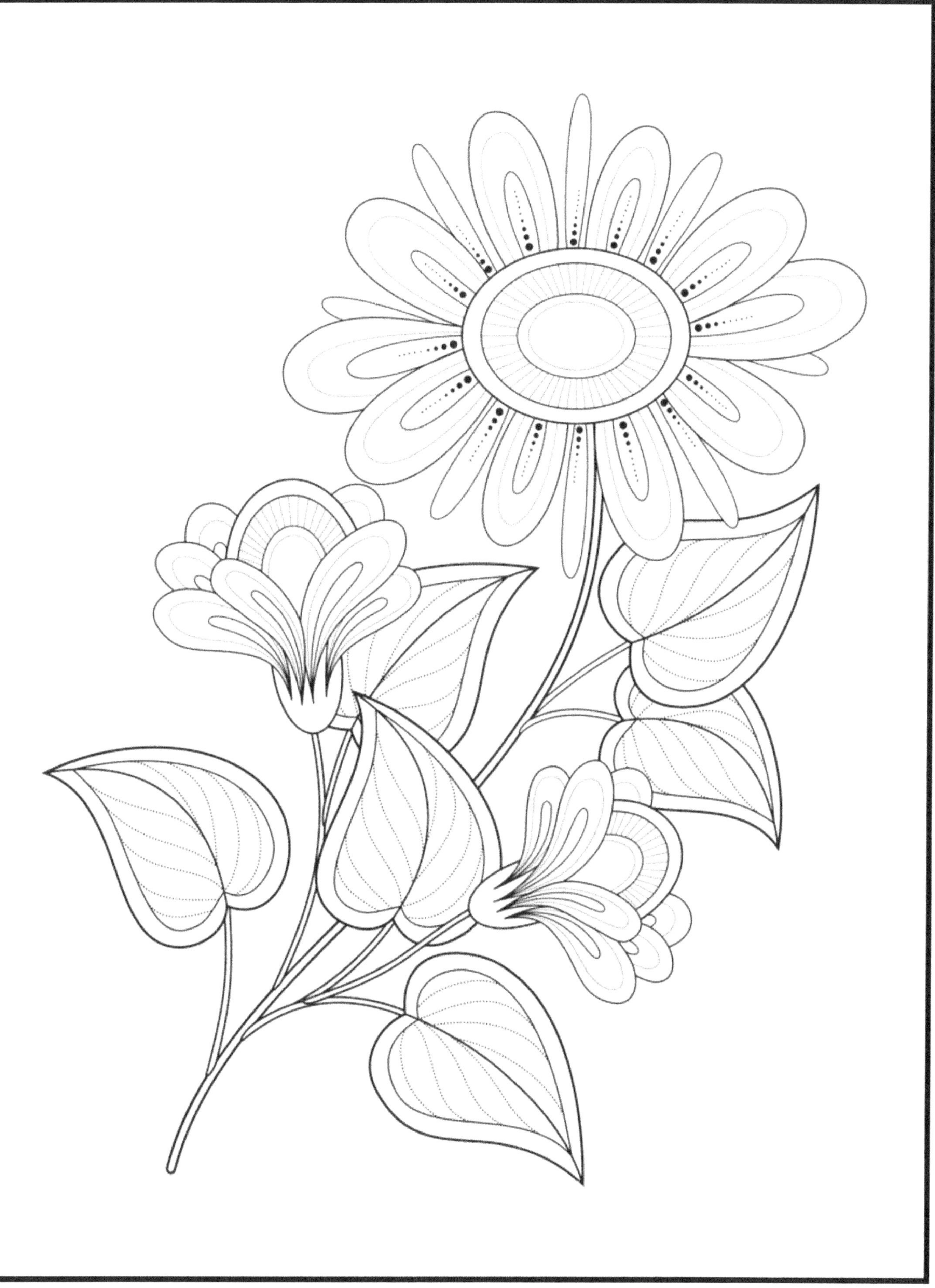

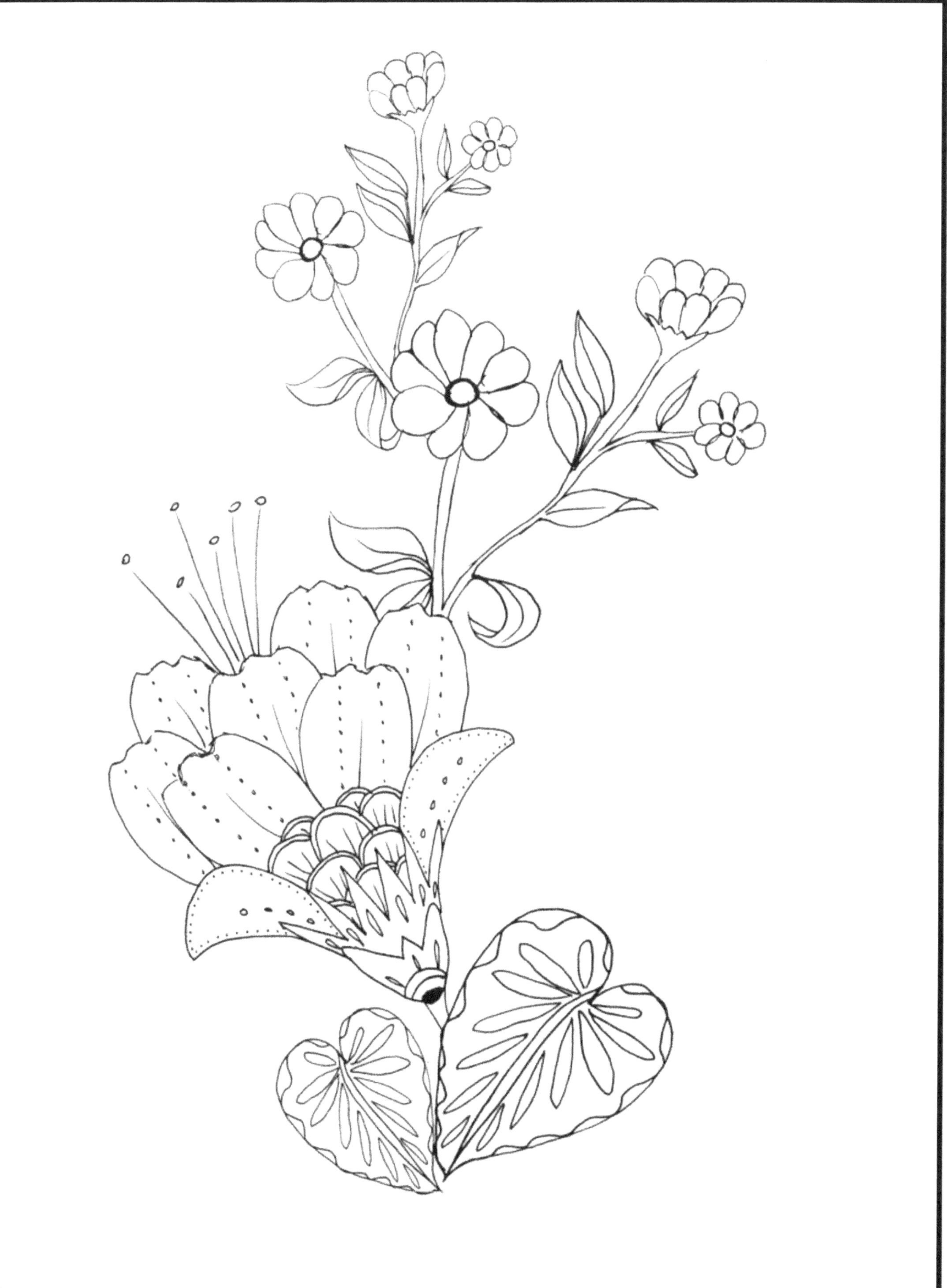